Thank you for
your support—Melissa.
A journey not shared is a sad
not healed. — D. Shaw [signature]
706.578.78

12

A Memoir
TO MY
YOUNGER SELF

SHANIQUA JONES

SHANIQUA JONES PUBLISHING, LLC

12: A Memoir To My Younger Self

Books may be purchased by contacting the publisher and author at:

Shaniqua Jones Publishing, LLC – Shaniqua Jones
www.shaniquajones.com .

Cover & Interior Design: Julie M. Holloway, JMH Cre8ive Solutions

Editor: Tiffany Jasper, Tiff's Editing Café

Cover photo credit: Felice Kimbrew

ISBN:

978-1511565165

1. Self Help 2. Spirituality

First Edition

Printed in the United States

DO NOT ALLOW THE
SHACKLES OF YOUR PAST
IMPRISON YOU WHEN YOU
HAVE THE KEYS TO BREAK
FREE!

Shaniqua Jones

1/21/2016

Acknowledgments

To the soul sent by God, I cherish each moment with you for you changed my views on love and respect. You came into my life in 2006 and have remained committed to this process. Your word has and remains to be your bond. I appreciate you, Mr. Dedrick Jones, Sr. – my Earthly anchor. To my five children, you are the reason this memoir exists. To my babies, times have not always been the greatest, but knowing you are the reason why I keep pressing forward gives me strength. Over the years, I've learned plenty of life lessons that made me wonder why I had to be the one to experience certain trials. I finally figured it out. These life lessons learned were for me to teach you....teach you how to love yourself, the importance of self-care and respect, the levels of respect for others, and the benefits of living righteously…and that there are NO shortcuts to this journey.

I was not given a guide or a tutorial when I became a mother. I possess a foundation based on the love of God. I strayed for some time and experienced many hardships, yet I am still standing. Mama loves you forever. I love my children brought by love through our union. You will always hold a special place in my heart. God blessed me with the most loving and prayerful woman I have ever encountered. I call her Jesus little sister, my mama, Evangelist Odia B. Anderson. Ma, I thank you for showing authentic, unconditional love. In memory of my father, Mr. Leo W. Anderson…I will always be your little Señorita. You left this world in 2003. I still had questions. God provided all the answers. I am blessed to have three brothers who took on the task of raising me. Thank you Levert, Roderick, and Delmar. To my mother-in-love, Ms.

Pearl Jones, I love you so much for being real in the rawest form. I thank you for checking me when needed. To my sisters-in-laws, nieces, nephews, cousins, my blood, and even my water…I love you! For everyone I met through my journey, I thank you!

Dr. Lynette L. Danley, you have challenged me to the fullest as my doctoral committee chair. Thank you. Dr. James Coldren (Pops), thank you for stirring up a gift I thought I had lost. Restorative Justice is our justice. Dr. Aurelio Valente, as a mentor, professor, and dean you managed to respond to my many requests as you saw fit. Thanks! Dr. Marlon Cummings, you stepped in right on time to provide the balance I needed to complete this portion of my academic studies. I appreciate you.

Love to my Faith Movers and Governors State University families!

Excuses are monuments of nothingness. They build bridges to nowhere. Those of us who use these tools of incompetence, seldom become anything but nothing at all. ~ Author Unknown

TO WHOM MUCH IS GIVEN, MUCH IS REQUIRED ~ LUKE 12:48

Chapter One

1 Ingalls Drive

From 1980 – 2006, this place has given me a sense of life and death. I was born November 22, 1980, to Mr. & Mrs. Leo W. Anderson at Ingalls Memorial Hospital in Harvey, Illinois. I can recall visiting this place for vaccination purposes during my childhood. I am so glad I never had a fear of needles. I had this idea that every time I visited the doctor's office, needles were involved. Sounds corny, I know.

But from my days at the pediatrician to adulthood, over the years, life changing situations occurred that molded me into the woman I am today; Dr. Shaniqua Jones.

There are some sensitive moments during my life and I want to prepare you for what I have to share. There is no filter and I chose this piece of written expression in hopes of someone being healed from sharing my journey.

Enough with the mushy intro to my happily ever after. Let's get right to it. Patricia; born in 1998. Patrick in 2000, Ayanna in 2004, Ariel in 2005, and Sanaa in 2006. All five children were born at Ingalls Memorial Hospital. I gave birth to five children over the course of eight years. The last three children were born in less than three years…WOW! I was a lost soul.

I thought if I gave my all, including my vajayjay (vagina) love was inevitable. We'll dig deeper into the whole idea of giving up your precious jewels in another chapter.

In the summer of 2002 I found myself in a dark place. I attempted to commit suicide. I had no hope, will, or desire to live. I was a mother of two children by a young man who I trusted to guard my heart and would make any sacrifice to be my forever. I assumed that because he was my love; my first love who I thought had me at my prime; slimmer, full of life, contagious smile, and attractive in every way possible (my point-of-  view). I imagined there was no way he would leave me. I was goofy and still naïve. I had no clue about life. I just wanted to be a 'car booty', ride nice, and raise my daughter.

The friends I shared my childhood with had no children. They 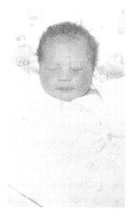 were either going off to college, working full-time jobs, or living what I thought to be a more spontaneous life. I, on the other hand, was at home with my mother who I rebelled against, the brothers who visited, and the constant reminders of the poor choices I had made. I became the neighborhood chick a.k.a. Qua-Qua who wanted to hang out all night long and participate in all types of proscribed activities. I wanted to feel a void…it didn't happen. Even through the hardships of attempting to maintain an unhealthy relationship, we raised our daughter as irresponsible young parents. We both had a mentality of being spoiled and did not take full responsibility for the child we made together.

 Although we were no longer together, we still had casual sex and as long as I made myself available to him…well, you know… I had got to the point where I thought I was grown even though I still lived under my mother's roof. I honestly believe once a young lady turns 18 and begin to live irresponsibly, she needs to move out of her parent's home. In my case, I became too grown for my own good and my mother had no choice but to put me out of her home. I was out of control, disrespectful, and did not want to follow her rules. I left with two bags and a child in my arms. I walked to a nearby friend's home until the only person I could call would come and save me because I allowed my rebellion and pride to overtake my need to respect the one person who cared for me more than God; my mother. I called my child's father. Without going into too much detail, Patrick was conceived in this process. I gave birth to my only born son, Patrick Odell High on October 26, 2000. Because of the dynamics of not being in an official relationship, my son was initially denied as being my children's father own flesh and blood. That was a low blow and sometimes the people we care about the most

will disappoint us with their actions of carelessness or dismissal.

You better make sure you find love within. If you are searching for someone to complete you or to fulfill your heart desires, you lose yourself in someone else who may not have your best interest at heart. I understand my children's father wanting definite answers, especially when we were no longer in a "committed" relationship (which really never existed). Yet, I was so lost that I could not see nor comprehend the reason at the time, but when you are blinded by lust masked by love, you cannot see anything clearly.

Fast forward.

I thought I had reached my lowest low. One night after hanging in the park with my babies and friends, I came home exhausted and full of tears. The struggle was so real at home that my mother and I did not have enough to buy a pack of pampers for my one-year-old son. This was not my mother's responsibility, but her being the unapologetically loving and supportive mother she is she made great sacrifices even in the midst of my destruction. Mind you, I stated mother and me (I) which meant I returned home even more broken than I was before and my mother allowed me to return. It  was so hot in the house that we had to borrow a fan from a neighbor. Being from a town where you are constantly reminded of who you were and what you have become, I felt thwarted. I wanted to take my life and end it all. I had become the young lady I did not want to be. The baby mama. The ghetto girl with no aspirations in life who lives on public assistance month-to-month.

While I am suffering in silence, the one I gave my heart to move on with his life and I couldn't accept it. I had planned to live my life with him. I gave up a full scholarship to study journalism in order to be a family to my then unborn first child and boyfriend. I strayed from my home to be under him. I never planned a life without him. I made attempts to bounce back and take college classes and work part-time. I wanted to regain my confidence, but never changed my surroundings which led to a deeper sorrow.

I overdosed on my mother's pain killers and alcohol I got from  a friend's house and drifted off to hell while holding my son. I thought by the time my mother realized her medicine was missing, it would be too late. Vaguely, I remember my mother rushing into my bedroom to find me and my son dripping wet in my bed. I can hear her yelling my name. I can feel her shaking me in hopes I would come to. My mother called the ambulance and my youngest brother and his wife. At the time, my brother and his wife lived 10 minutes away from our mother's home. My brother and his wife beat the ambulance's arrival.

My brother has always been the laid back, chill type of guy. He rarely raised his voice or quick to anger. He is tall and slim in stature. He slapped the shit out of me and still no sudden response. He and his wife drove me to Ingalls Hospital straight to the emergency room where I was questioned:

"What is your name? What is your date of birth? Where are you right now? Do you know why you are here?"

I did not know any of the answers and was going in and out of consciousness. The nurse shoved a tube down my throat while I was restrained on a gurney. The nurses had to pump my stomach and coat with charcoal. The amount of pain killers and alcohol caused my liver to collapse. I had to be admitted to spend additional time in the hospital. Can you imagine my state-of-mind? I had no clue who cared for my children or where they were. I should have thought of that before the failed attempt. Dumb. For my mother to be the one who found me as I laid in complete sorrow and facing death…brings me to tears as I write.

For the first few days, I had to consume charcoal. As time progressed, I was able to eat the bare minimum. I talked to my

mother every day. After spending approximately a week in the hospital, I told my mom that I heard the news that I was getting ready to be discharged. Yay! Right?

Nope. I was discharged from the hospital and transferred through this underground tunnel on a gurney to the mental health facility, the Wyman & Gordon building. The underground tunnel reminds me of the one from my  senior year of high school when I switched homerooms when administration learned I was pregnant.

This was the worst. What I didn't realize was that my attempt or cry for attention was more than just a stay in the hospital. It meant I had to seek professional help. While on my mini vacation to this secluded location, I met some interesting people who probably thought the same thing about me. As patients we had no control of the blinds, water to shower, or switches.

We ate as a family; a family of perfect strangers. We all took our medication at the same time to keep us balanced. Well....everyone except me. I held my pill under my tongue until the nurse moved on to the next person. As soon as she turned away, I would place the pill on my fork and mix in with my veggies and notify the staff that I was done eating.

I participated in group activities that pulled the creativity of each one of us. I drew and painted two art pieces while on vacation. I realized I had lost over 40 pounds in a three week time frame. That is probably because I wouldn't eat my food, or had become active, and was missing my mom and babies. Then the time came where I needed to meet with the psychiatrist. He asked me basic questions that I later realized were more complex, leading to his observations of my mental state.

He diagnosed me with bi-polar disorder. I always heard (once I became a 'rebel'), "that girl is crazy!" I guess they may have been on to something. NOT!

One of the most hurtful feelings was being given a limit and specific time to talk to my mom and babies on the phone. My daughter asking me when I was coming home and my son's jibber jabber sounds melodic to my ears yet emotional. I didn't have the answers and then the call ends abruptly. The staff yells and notifies the patients in the ward to get ready to report to our rooms and go to bed. I felt like I was a cast member of Orange is the New Black.

When I was released into the care of my Aunt Mary and Aunt Liz; I asked where my mother was. Moms' was at home with my two babies. Once we got home, it wasn't like graduating from college or coming home after serving in the Armed Forces. There wasn't a swarm of people waiting in the driveway when I got out the car. Who was present were my two praying aunts, my babies, and my mom. They prayed a powerful prayer of deliverance.

Over the course of the next two weeks, my mom maintained all of my motherly duties as I sat still in the living room high on medication. I was emotionless. I was catatonic in a closet.

We never had a serious conversation about mental illness and how my issues affect my children. I was 21 years old when I was diagnosed with bipolar disorder. My mama took me off the medication that had me bound. I showed no emotion even in times of a crisis. One of the disheartening realities I learned after his passing was that my father was diagnosed as schizophrenic. Not to excuse my own illness, I wanted to touch on the subject of the research suggesting a relation of mental illness within the bloodline.

In the Black community, we brush mental illness off by jokingly calling someone crazy and off the chain when in actuality there may be some underlying issues such as mental illness. I have caught myself in the act of ridiculing someone when I should be the one who understands the reason for the excess behavior. I don't condone suicide whatsoever yet we have to be clear on what is needed in this individual's life – we have to show more love and compassion. We have to seek healing to provide the space for others to heal as well.

Fast forward.

After giving birth to my second child at the age of 19, I began to have abnormal pap smears which led to my fear and inconsistency to schedule necessary doctor appointments. It seems as if when you are feeling terrible, the doctor doesn't see anything wrong. When you are feeling great and can conquer the world is when the doctor always have some unsatisfying news that you do not want to hear.

The worst thing you can do is to not participate in tending to your healthcare needs. You have to be mentally and physically present when you visit your doctor. When the doctor explains something you do not understand, ask questions. The worst question is the question not asked. Do not feel slighted or intimidated when you encounter difficulties in expressing yourself. Always seek knowledge in every situation you encounter.

I stopped going to the doctor because I assumed time and prayer would heal all wounds. True in many situations yet negligence only led to a life altering situation. I learned I had cervical cancer via Human Papillomavirus (HPV) towards the end of 2005. To me, all I could register in my small mindedness was HPV sounding so close to HIV.....WHAT? Not to mention, I was pregnant with my fourth child and married to someone who was addicted to drugs. Too much happening at one time!

I blamed myself for not taking the necessary precautions due to my ignorance. I did not see the physical effects of the abnormal pap smears so I kept it moving. Plus, I did not take the doctors seriously when explaining how abnormal pap smears if untreated could lead to more serious medical concerns. I had no real support system after damaging the family dynamics that I had known all my life. And again, I will cover this topic in another chapter. Once I made contact with my mother to explain the severity of the situation, we all came together in support of facing cancer head on. While many speak of the praying grandmother, I speak of the praying mother.

I sought treatment (not chemotherapy) and prayer to face the attack on my body and was healed. As of spring 2016, I am 11 years cancer-free! A victory added to my life!

No matter what the circumstances, God will see you through.

Darkness is only temporary. Life is precious and should be valued as a creation of God; one of God's greatest creations. One of a kind. When you are feeling down and in despair, you better pray. One of the worst things you can do is speak negatively of your situation to someone whose been waiting on this moment. There are people that have a certain image of you  that makes them feel comfortable. They wait for you to encounter a critical situation in hopes that image remains just that, if not worse. Don't let your image become greater than they imagined. They'll want you to revert back to that image and dog you out in the process.

You are never alone. God is with you. There were times I shared my sorrows with the wrong individual believing that I was alone. God has always been there even through the  tumultuous times. Ask God for the spirit of discernment to have the innate ability to know the difference between those who love you and those who despise you. Ask God to move the mountain or give you the strength to climb. Do not take life for granted. Each day given is another opportunity, another chance.

Two subjects I have discussed are suicide and cervical cancer.

I am providing the National Suicide Prevention Lifeline number: 1-800-273-TALK (8255). For more information on HPV, go to: http://www.cdc.gov/std/hpv/stdfact-hpv.htm (Center for Disease Control and Prevention).

People of all ages, ethnicity, characteristics, and demographics are leaving this place. I suggest we get our houses in order for this minute, hour, day, or tomorrow is not promised.

Matthew 24:36 (NIV) But about that day or hour no one knows, not even the angels in heaven, nor the Son, but only the Father.

Chapter Two

159ᵀᴴ & CARSE/WOODBRIDGE

This is the second place I could actually call home; the first being my mother's womb. #HarveyWorld, born and raised. I am not ashamed of where I come from. Corruption exists everywhere! We were one of the only Black families in this neighborhood. I thought we were the perfect family from what I can recall. I was loved by a mother and father, three teen brothers ranging from the ages of 13-17 (in 1980). I was the only girl. My daddy gave me the name Senorita before I could

even walk. Oh! When I did learn how to maneuver around the house, I tore some stuff up. My daddy said I was entitled to do whatever I wanted because it was my house. I would walk into my brother's room and knock EVERYTHING off their dressers. Ruthless! Lol!

In some ways, I feel his actions set me up for failure as I believed that I could have anything I wanted just from the idea of wanting it alone.

My daddy really means something special to me. He was my world. That world was short lived. What I was not exposed to was the other side of him that dealt with or the inability to deal with his anger issues and unresolved childhood issues. Nonetheless, he will always be my father, my daddy! What I learned from this situation was that no matter what he did or how he may have treated people, he was still human. We tend to forget our own faults when addressing others pitfalls. Who are we to judge?

Oftentimes, we fail to look beyond or delve deeper into the heart and soul because our emotions drive us to anger or hate. People do not act out for no reason. There is always an underlying issue covering a cry for help or attention. We also have to realize that self-care is vital to living this life. We have to know when to stay and when to let go. We cannot allow the mishaps of others to prevent us from living a life more pleasing to God.

It's safe to say that this was the beginning to a long end as one family unit. My oldest brother was preparing to leave for college while the two other brothers were getting older and roles changed where the middle boy became the oldest,  responsible son as well as my mother's protector. We all have a special bond with our mother but the middle son matured on a different level. Maybe I should back up a little. Our family dynamics are blended where my mother birthed four children; the two oldest boys having a different father. My father had three (that we know of) children from his first marriage. I know there may be more. It's possible. Blended families are more known than we tend to believe. These special blends started way before the term was coined.

From the many stories we share within our immediate family, I learned the racial tension in Harvey, Illinois in the 80s were prominent. Blacks were not truly welcomed; especially in the first ward. While some of these areas were becoming more integrated, the first ward was holding on to an all-White culture as long as they could.

My family experienced our garage being vandalized with the words, MOVE NIGGERS painted on the garage. After overcoming that obstacle, my family decided to stay nonetheless. They were not going to be bullied and pushed out of their home. Many  thought we lived a high maintenance life not knowing the abuse my mother and brothers faced on a daily basis. Many abusers have been abused themselves and lack the support needed to resolve their own personal obstacles which prolong the healing process if there is ever one to begin or end with.

 Unresolved issues and loneliness can cause a prolonged period of pain which can lead to a lifetime of pain if one does not seek God for healing. This is what I understand marriage to be: a union brought by God in order to fulfill His purpose and will for your life, the lives of your children, and for generations to come. What I have come to realize is the need for attention and affection in times of despair can lead you into the arms of the enemy. This God-given spouse is to be loved and cherished until you take your last breath. Let us be mindful that the last breath you take is not to be by the one you love. I believe it is safe to say that if God sent this person to you – this is NEVER a worry you have to face.

Love is patient. Love is kind. It does not envy, it does not boast, it is not proud. It does not dishonor others, it is not self-seeking, it is not angered, and it keeps no record of wrongs. Love does not delight in evil but rejoices with the truth. It always protects, always trusts, always hopes, and always preserves ~ I Corinthians 13:4-7.

I talked about love but never explained lust. Lust is temporary with only one emotion to fulfill a sexual desire. Sex isn't love and neither is lust. Trying to convince yourself to love someone when it's an attraction, a sinful temptation only creates more havoc in your life. For a lack of better explanation, lust makes you feel good in the moment but you lack authentic concern for the other person. You'll find yourself lost in the scheme of things quickly. Lust will cause you to lose focus of the path God has for you. We are human and have the desire to be wanted and accepted, but at what cost? Do you want to be used and abused before finding the one God had for you all along? Do you want to be so broken to the point where no relationship lasts longer than a television series?

These are just a few of the questions you should ask. On a deeper level, do you want to experience bouts with fatal

diseases because your desire to sleep with someone was so strong that you had unprotected sex? Be careful. Guard your body. I can recall my mother telling me when she felt I was old enough to understand that she made the decision to leave my father so I would not think abuse was the norm. Although I may not have seen my father hit my mother, I do recall many heated arguments that led to noise behind closed doors.

My father kept a loaded gun in the house to intimidate my two oldest brothers. Sad. I climbed the dresser and pulled the gun out. Nosey. Thank God my mother walked in just in time to take the gun from me. It was time to move out of this chaotic situation.

I can remember the day my mother moved to 16320 Carse Avenue. Because of my relationship with my daddy, I was sent to my Aunt Bea home for the day to make sure I did not tell my daddy of our new whereabouts.

God intervened on that day as He is known to do. The fight my mother thought her and my brothers were going to face did not occur. My daddy actually offered a bit of advice on how to properly store furniture on the moving truck. My daddy's issues with the need to control and live a life attempting to live up to another man's legacy

destroyed the family dynamics. My mother's first husband was a true gentleman and my mother suffered in silence when he passed away. The image she remembers is nowhere remotely close to the feelings she has for my father. My father may have tried to diminish that image or may have even been envious.

He took his anger out on those who loved him beyond his external image. Even though my parents separated when I was six years old, they never divorced. They made attempts to reestablish or rekindle old flames, but those attempts were always short lived.

Abuse comes in many forms and we tend to turn the other cheek because the receiving of the abuse derives from a person we love. The issue of remaining in a chaotic and abusive relationship is that the situation does not get any better. No form of abuse is acceptable and is not to be  tolerated in any household. Whether it is physical, mental, financial, or any other form, speak out. Do not silence the pain. Do not allow the pain someone is experiencing cause you to be the punching bag to relieve them of their frustrations.

The day could come where you are no longer here to share your story.

Unfortunately, I faced abuse firsthand with my ex-husband. I will admit that I played my part in the abuse because I had to fend for myself. I had to protect my children. My craziness and foul way of thinking began to enjoy fighting someone I allowed to tear me down. I was broken and out of my mind. Violence is never the answer. I am thankful to still be here. My life had become a Lifetime Movie and the saga (marriage) continued for five consecutive years; 2003-2008. He still made attempts to cause havoc in my life after our 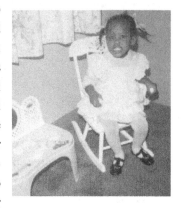 divorce. The beginning was pure bliss covered by the darkness of lust, drugs, and family dysfunction. We jeopardize the lives of all those involved when we partake in the ills of abuse.

I have come to realize the calling on my mother's life allowed her to not only go through, but to get through to help her only daughter, me. The calling on her life brought her to a place of healing through forgiveness. Her obedience to God has helped others in their personal journeys to overcome many life obstacles. Forgive without hesitation. I know it sounds easy but just keep living. The more pain and resentment you harbor the more sluggish you are and you lose your inner and outer beauty. Harboring past hurts and pains will only cause you grief and mental anguish.

Let go. Let God.

Love - love everything about you from your hair or the lack thereof to your unique smile. Always walk with your head held high with proper structure. Fall so deep in love with yourself so you'll know and expect to be treated right. I mentioned the journey early on and have to admit that the journey is to be respected. The lessons you learn while on your journey will help you understand yourself as an individual. A profound scholar once shared these simple yet complex in fulfilling words, "if these problems were easy, they'll be fixed." Tough love has made me a stronger parent whose maturity derives from displaying  true concern for your well being. To my babies, I may have been too silly or too lax when it came to maintaining a relationship with you. I had to understand that I am not your friend. We can have a friendly and trusting relationship without crossing the line of being your equal. Sounds confusing. Keep living and you'll begin to see where I'm coming from. I'm coming from a place of love.

 Domestic violence is a pattern of physical and psychological abuse, threats, intimidation, isolation or economic coercion used by one person to exert power and control over another person in the context of dating, family, or household relationship. Domestic violence is maintained by societal and cultural attitudes, institutions and laws which are not consistent with

naming this violence as wrong ~ South Suburban Family Shelter, Inc.
For more information about South Suburban Family Shelter, go to: http://www.ssfs1.org/

Chapter Three

6028 S. CHAMPLAIN

God is real. I was born and raised Church Of God In Christ (COGIC); Freedom Temple COGIC to be exact. I was named Lil' Missionary after the congregation because many saw what I felt in my soul even through my stages of denial and rebellion. By the time my mother realized she was pregnant with me, her life began to shift into a more spiritual realm. She was filled with the Holy Spirit while she carried me. The wife and mother my father and brothers once knew no longer existed. She was renewed and restored.

The Holy Spirit brought about a change in her life that prepared her for the ministry of supporting and guiding women who experienced life trials and tribulations without support. The nine fruits of the Holy Spirit are exemplified in her walk with Christ:

- Love
- Joy
- Peace
- Longsuffering
- Kindness
- Goodness
- Faithfulness
- Gentleness
- Self-control

But the fruit of the Spirit is love, joy, peace, longsuffering, kindness, goodness, faithfulness, gentleness, self-control ~ Galatians 5:22

I can only share the journey I know and witnessed. I can recall not being able to wear pants, red polish, lipstick or colored lip gloss, ear piercings, or short hair...ha ha ha ha! I guess that answers the question as to why I continue to wear short hair. Unfortunately, I thought any one of the above was a sin and an abomination of God. I am so glad to know that I am learning

God for myself and cannot define my salvation by religion but by my personal walk with Him. I see the dedication and sacrifice many make to belong in the church. We struggled and went without basic necessities at times, yet we tithed and

 volunteered for many functions at the church. I could not fathom the idea of serving a God who knew our struggles and did not protect us from the ills of financial strain and poverty. Keep living!

Many times pride prevented us from seeking the help we needed as well as the help we knew we could get from those who loved us. Every time I began to question God (which I was taught never to do), a blessing would occur. One of the members would bless us with a love token or pay for me to attend a youth retreat. If I wanted to participate in any activity, it would be paid in full without ever knowing whose act of kindness it was. There were times my school supplies were purchased by one of the saints. Trips and competitions I wanted to participate in were paid for.

COGIC is known for the dancing and hollering church...as I could recall. I never delved into true worship. I thought the only way to rejoice and communicate with God is to be loud and overbearing. It took some trials as a young adult to understand the concept of worship and how to reach God through prayer. The power of prayer is life changing. Don't get me wrong, my spiritual foundation always kept me grounded even in my chaos. I knew God had a hold of me early on. I knew at the age of 15 when I began to rebel and publically asked to go through in order to have a powerful testimony later in life, I was going to get exactly what I asked. God is not a game. He is not to be taken for granted. He saw the best in me even when I could not see the slightest good in myself.

One of my struggles with religion is that its comparison is the same effect the gang affiliations or how economic status has to divide and conquer is equal in many aspects. I witnessed the struggle of acceptance when my mother was called to preach. God called her but man gave her a position in the church that was deemed suitable by leadership, or just rejected her request.

There comes a time in our life when we have to understand that the calling God places on your life will not be accepted by those we love and those who we believe love us. We cannot continue to be a vessel of Christ in fear of being unaccepted or ridiculed. God never gives us any more than we can handle. Never! One of the greatest lessons I learned is that tradition is repetitive yet does not make act of tradition right. We have to be radical for Christ! It is not about the color of our skin, the economic status, the clothes we wear, the hairstyle of choice, or any other material aspect. Now, I am a Faith Mover.

I gave every breathing moment to my church home because that was all I knew. I was my mother's protégé. Her circle of friends consisted of my Aunt Lorene and Missionary Pearson who were both older than her. Let me remind you that she had me at the age of 40! Here I am no more than five or six years old hanging with women of God ten times my age or more. Our typical Sunday schedule was to pick up breakfast for Sunday School, arrive to church before anyone else except one faithful deacon, serve breakfast, participate in Sunday School, enjoy a15-minute break between morning service and afternoon service, attend afternoon service which lasted about 3 to 3.5 hours, talk to everyone after service, go to dinner at Glady's (an old soul food restaurant which was one of my mom's first jobs when she migrated from Mississippi to Chicago), go to night service (YPWW), and then to take my aunt home. Our Sunday started at 6:30 am and would not end until after midnight (most Sunday's).

I have not even covered the other six days of the week. There was Tuesday morning prayer in the summer months. There was Wednesday night Bible study. There were frequent Friday night services or events. Saturday, was youth choir rehearsal or volunteering our time.

I have a god-mother who was not on of my mother's sisters. (All my other god-mothers were my mom's sisters). She came along and nurtured me when my mother's health became challenging. To this day, I owe her an apology because when I disappeared from the church, I disappeared from her life as well. Actually, anyone who was associated with this particular church, I deliberately broke ties. She never had a biological daughter but she treated me like I was her own flesh and blood. I was her personal baby doll. Awh!

There was a family that took me in as their own when I was in middle school and high school. They meant the world to me. Between my god-mother's home and this family's home, these were the only two places I could spend the night out. My mama did not play those "you spend the night out at people's house" games. Nope! Not Evangelist Odia B. Anderson. She was not going!

The moment I began to feel myself or smell myself like my mom would say, I rebelled against everything instilled in me.

Before the new school year, the church would have a special youth service praying over all of us and asking God to protect us as we go to and from our destinations. This one particular service, I was preparing to enter high school and one of the greatest missionaries ever asked one simple yet complex question, "Lil' Missionary, do you want to be saved?" Here I am standing in front of the congregation along the side of other

 friends (youth of the church) as they answered yes...I think more because they were afraid to reply any other way and rightfully speaking, that was right, right? My reply, "No ma'am." I think I felt the heat from my mother's eyes on the back of my neck. This is the moment I became the rebel. Lil' Missionary was gone forever. Now, let me be real for a minute, I have never hated God or even despised God when I thought I was going through but here I am 14 or 15 years old and have convinced my mother to buy me these colored contacts, perm and style my hair into an appropriate hairstyle, lost the baby fat...and you want fine ole me to get saved??? Baby bye! Moms taught me to be true to God and to myself and I may have taken that a step further but I was true and still am. If I have some reservation regarding a matter whether the truth hurts or not, you will know.

God is not pleased when we hurt others and this is why it is important to operate in the nine fruits of the Holy Spirit. There is a term called tactfulness which means to be appropriate in the way you communicate (verbal and non-verbal) with others. There is a time and place for everything even in times we are put on the spot; we have to ask God to guide our words.

Unfortunately, the moment I began to stray there were not too many saints there to guide me into the right direction. There were some waiting on me to fail while others wanted to stay clear of the troubled child. Recently my pastor, Pastor Moses Herring brought a message about the leper who sought Jesus

 and was cleansed by Him. Jesus set the example of how we should treat people who suffer from things seen and unseen yet are always shunned away. If you do not look like the crowd or operate like the crowd, you are ostracized. I no longer had the desire to attend church in search of what I thought I was missing in the world. As a result, I began to hang with a crowd unbecoming.

Some of my church friends who were really concerned about me would come looking for me to attend a youth service or revival.

I strayed and wanted to be someone I was not. Not too long after straying away from the only structure I knew, I was a 17-year-old lost soul, pregnant with my first child. If I wasn't accepted for being the mouthy rebel, I'm sure I don't think I am going to be accepted now either. I noticed I was fine once my mother came to terms of our reality.

One night my dear friend who knew me well since we grew up in church together and attended all four years of high school together, stopped by and asked me to attend a revival service. Because of her sincerity, I rode to church with her. I sat on the last row (the sinner's row...jokingly). The well-known preacher had the church on fire and the anointing was so high that I began to rock and cry hysterically. I immediately caught myself because shame overcame me and I allowed the devil to kill my moment of peace and joy.

The preacher spoke a Word like I never heard before and his message spoke volumes relating to the leper, acceptance, and forgiveness. You know we go to church in our times of despair and know the message was for us as if the preacher walked a mile in our shoes. All of a sudden, the preacher jumped out of the pulpit and sped right to me. He shouted, "Chocolate Wonder, don't you ever forget who you are and whose you are!" I can't remember everything but that stuck with me.

The closer I got to giving birth to my first born, I began to draw weary of people I disappointed and the promising future I could no longer have...

I gave birth to my first child, Patricia Odia High on Friday, October 9, 1998, at 8:42pm. She weighed 7lb. 11oz. 21in. Although I gave birth to her, she was the prettiest baby I had ever laid eyes on. God gave her to me.

Six weeks to the day, I turned 18 years old. I had Patricia christened on my 18th birthday. What was to be one of the most important days of my life as I reached a new level of maturity or so I thought, was a day to remember in a sensitive way. Because I could not choose one brother over the other, I decided to have all three of my brothers as  godparents to my baby girl along with their spouses. Patricia's father chose his two siblings as well. So here we have this untraditional christening ceremony before the entire congregation where my former pastor left me feeling helpless. I know he is human and has flaws as well, but he made it his point to share his personal feelings of the high hopes many of the congregation had for me and how I let him down. This alone was the reason why I decided to leave and never return to church. Church is to be a place of deliverance not a place to provoke anger.

The lesson I learned was to never rely on man, for man alone cannot sustain your spiritual growth. You are to solely rely on God and His promises for your life. You cannot worship man for you will be greatly disappointed. Your faith and trust should be in God alone and ask him to give you the wisdom and discernment to know what decisions you need to make. 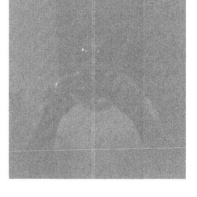 I had to learn and relearn this concept because I was too heart-headed to walk the path I knew to walk. Believe me, the path chosen nor the path God provided will not be easy, but will be well worth the wait. He will give you the desires of your heart... Trust in the LORD with all thine heart; and lean not unto thine own understanding ~ Proverbs 3:5.

When it is all said and done, you must have a personal relationship with God and you cannot allow people to deter you from serving Him. I know at some point you will experience spiritual freedom, but knowing what we have been through together and what I have shared with you, know He holds our future.

You do not need an audience to worship. You do not need to be in the brick and mortar to accept Christ. You do not have to quote scriptures or hoot and holler to hear from Him. He is wherever you are. You are never alone.

I've struggled in all of my relationships with those I love due to not taking the necessary precautions and time to understand what triggers my emotions. Growing up in the church and praying through and for breakthroughs hindered my ability to seek professional help. God is real and evident in my life to the point where I've accepted the fact that professional help is perfectly fine. As long as we remain conscious of who holds our future and to not worship man for their gifts, we are headed in the right direction.

The love I have for my children grows deeper than any sea and beyond the vivid skies. I honestly couldn't imagine life without them. They are one of the reasons God allows me to breathe. God is amazing and will be the greatest friend you'll ever have. Pray every night and each morning. Pray during every moment you have an opportunity to do so! Meditate....take the time to reflect and appreciate the greatness of each day and the areas of improvement.

Another thing, make your own money to sustain you for the long run. Learn to live by the 70/20/10 rule of your income; 70% spend, 20% save, and 10% tithes. You'll save yourself some headaches. God will always provide and take care of His children.

You know how I tell you to, 'let go and let God'...well do just that! Practice this as much as possible and the task in doing so will become a part of your lifestyle.

My decision

I have decided to become part of God's family by asking Jesus to make my heart new and become Lord of my life.
From now on I want to serve God by following His ways and doing what He wants me to do.

Name: ....

Date: ....

Date of the decision (if you know it).

Chapter Four

BRITTANY WOODS

Disclaimer: very short period in my life..
.filled with life lessons

Funny thing is that I drive past this apartment complex every Sunday on my way to and from church. I loved my Barbie doll house my parents bought me along with the White Barbie doll and Black Michael Jackson figure. They were a perfect match, if you asked me. I was color blind and I genuinely loved everyone. I was in love with the Transformers, too. I had a child-size Transformer that matched me in height. Oh! Let's not forget Betty! I miss my boo! Betty was a life-size baby doll with pretty brown eyes. I loved putting mounds of Vaseline in her hair to give her the lustrous silky look that we now pay hundreds of dollars for. Well....the hundreds of dollars you spend because I do NOT have it like that, lol.

I had the best of times playing as a child should. I may not have understood the dynamics of my parent's separation, but I had all the love I needed. The arguments I would casually hear from time to time between my mom and dad ceased. The one thing I knew, the separation brought joy to my mother's life. She smiled more. She praised God more openly. It's a shame that a man would prevent his wife from praising God too much because of his own insecurities. Some are jealous of the relationship women have with their Higher Power. So unfortunate. I am pretty sure my dad knew that once my mother grew tired of his mess, she would leave, and do so in peace.

Don't get me wrong, I love my daddy with all my heart and even through his craziness I still have mad respect for him even in his demise. He had a hustle mentality that no matter what line he walked, everything was alright. I could spend my life questioning the reasons why my parents made the decisions they made to separate rather than tough it out for the sake of saving face but quite a few of us would be in the grave. For a period of time, I blamed my mother for my own misbehavior because she made the most courageous decision ever to permanently leave my dad when we moved to 16320 Carse Avenue.

One too many times I have heard people close and afar make statements that they suffered their entire life because they lacked the structure needed in their own household as a child. Their mama or daddy abandoned them or someone suffered from addiction, poverty, lack of opportunity, or worse.

At what point in our lives do we take responsibility for our own  actions. There is only one person we can control – ourselves! We cannot change the dynamics of any situation as we entered into this world but what we can change is the way we think and the way we respond. I've been called a few things in my lifetime and always responded in a way that further removed me from the path of obtaining my goals. It's not what they call you but what you respond to! Once my mother was at peace with the name calling, bickering, and the dealings with instability that would probably rip a person's soul, she responded by choosing God wholeheartedly.

It's funny how all my life I went from admiring my mother to resenting her and now understanding all the life lessons she taught me along with facing some of my own challenges. The lessons she tried to teach me only drew me to those same ills she protected me from. I loved everything about her because I was her running buddy when she was not at work. The changes she made in our life were to provide peace in the midst of a storm I had no clue was in full motion. When we moved to Brittany Woods in University Park from Harvey, IL I thought we were in another state. Nothing was conveniently located.

Transition. What led us to Brittany Woods was that my mom decided to make the move. She felt a separation was best especially now that the two oldest are no longer living with us. The two oldest boys are now adults in college or working. They are grown now. It is just the three of us; mom, my youngest brother, and me. I can recall this one time when my mother took me for a walk in our complex. I thought I was too cute this particular day. Moms loved dressing me like a little ole' church lady. I could only wear skirts. I went to a Christian-based school; Christian Cornerstone in South Chicago Heights, Illinois. There were two boys watching us from a window and I stared back at them. They must have thought I was cute too! I fell down and rolled into a ditch. Even at that time, I felt it priceless having time with my mother. We still laugh about this to this day.

Due to our household dynamics having such a dramatic change, I expected a significant distance between me and my mother, but we became even closer. The youngest boy became my best friend during this period of time. Once he would get home from school, my mother would be able to rest before she went to work at a state facility overnight. We walked everywhere from his friend's house to the complex club house. Where we lived caused us to walk quite a distance just to go to the White Hen Pantry. He loves playing basketball and is very competitive. He may be laid back in nature but he's on the basketball court, he is in a zone.

All that walking we did then is now a clear indication to me how I stayed small back then. Boy has times changed since then. Now, I have to take 30,000 steps a day with my Fitbit just to lose one pound. I love my Fitbit!

I learned that we hold on to unhealthy and ineffective relationships because it had become a part of our norm.....our tradition. Yet, transition from tradition can become overwhelming in just the idea alone. My dad was living a vicarious life while facing some health challenges. He fell ill and sought the affection needed from my mother who was still his wife, even through the separation.

Loyalty and love goes hand-in-hand that can easily be taken for granted by those who cannot grasp the understanding of these simultaneous actions. See, me? I wanted my mother and father to be together because my vision could not see the truth. They were in a very unhealthy relationship filled with hurt and pain. Marriage is more than a term used to exemplify a contractual agreement to be there for someone in sickness and health but rather an action to uphold the other through a spiritual connection with God. The ideology that individuals should remain married through thick and thin is a double-standard or should be based on an individual basis. Too many people suffer in silence because of the ole' tradition or they took a path not chosen by God. You can't straddle the fence. You either roll with God all the way or no way at all. Simply put, is this a marriage God ordained or one you chose for yourself?

For a while, life became a game of hide-and-seek. Everyone was hiding something. My mother hid her pain. She was hurting and the fact that she took my dad back during his time  of need made life even more painful for her. She wasn't your average church goer. What I mean by this is the fact she was authentic with her praise night and day. The person she had become was one who was the same in light as she was in darkness. Praise and worship is all she did. I used to wonder if she ever angered or despised anyone. If she did, I had no clue.

There is a difference between church folks and people of the Kingdom. Church folks wear a mask and although their intent is right, their ways are of the world. People of the Kingdom are worshippers and love Christ to the extent that they walk the path He has ordained.

She was and still is a true worshipper. She decided some time ago to walk with Jesus even if it meant removing certain people from her life. My dad was hiding his true feelings of disappointment knowing he had no intentions to do right by my mother but was too selfish to remove himself from the picture. He was confused. He wanted the wife and the family but the streets and the scheming ways overcame the goodness of his heart. The worst battle he ever faced was the battle within. Before the talk about my parents possibly coming back together, my youngest brother was now the oldest sibling in our house. He was responsible for caring for me while my mother worked tirelessly.

The time had come and my dad moved in with us. He had aged and his sickness began to show. He was taking multiple medications on a daily basis. He not only suffered physically, he suffered mentally as well. Whether he had a mild stroke, heart attack, or suffered as a severe diabetic, he continued to smoke cigarettes. He thought I did not know but he carried a distinctive smell. My youngest brother began to smell just like him. I told my mother that my brother was smoking cigarettes. In order for her to believe me, I had to share my investigative skills. I told her to smell the door knob to his bedroom door and she did. The door knob smelled just like Newport's.

My mother made every attempt to be there for someone who had abandoned her emotions and her freedom to live a righteous life. It is difficult to live for Christ when you live with the enemy. Moms wanted peace. I cannot peg my dad to be perfect but he fought internal demons that would not allow him to enjoy peace of mind. Childhood issues continuously resurfaced and manifested into anger as he aged. He will always hold a special place in my heart because as long as he lived, I always knew he loved me.

As I reflect on this short period of time in my life, what I take away is this life lesson:

You can't please everyone. You will lose yourself and eventually your life in these useless attempts. Better or worse does not mean that you settle for mediocre. I am glad I witnessed certain hardships in order to fully appreciate my older years. I watched a woman of faith make attempts to be led by tradition. Tradition does not mean the act thereof is right....

My mother made peace with a dead situation which allowed me to understand that both of my parents had flaws. We all do. Even through the craziness associated with toxic relationships, I watched my mother's faith shift from good to great. I thank them for these life lessons.

When a man's ways please the LORD, He makes even his enemies to be at peace with him ~ Proverbs 16:7

When a man's ways please the LORD, he maketh even his enemies to be at peace with him.
Proverbs 16:7 (KJV)

versaday.com

Chapter Five

16001 S. CARSE AVENUE

Holmes School is working hard to be our best at everything from ABC to XYZ. I will study hard and do my very best. To accomplish to succeed. We agree our motto be...Holmes...working hard to be our best. This was, and may still be our school mottos created by our music teacher, Mr. Williams.

This is my childhood grammar school from first to sixth grade. But the best principal of all time is Mr. Phillip Skubal. He was our White version of Joe Clark from the movie, Lean on Me. He knew every child, older siblings, mama, daddy, grandma, and neighbor. He would walk blocks after school to make sure each child made it home safely. There was no such thing as calling your home because it was handled like Olivia Pope would say... He had this foot long paddle that either had thick rubber bands on them or something similar. I nevern recalled him having to use it even though there  were horror stories about him using it on previous students. I doubt it! He never had to use it on me.

Mr. Skubal was the father figure to those who did not have a male figure in the household as well as those who had someone. My first grade teacher was a gem. She taught with passion and gentleness. I did not keep in contact with a few of my teachers, but I have managed to visit my alma mater from time-to-time. We also had the best school secretary who never aged. Ms. Farfan, the school secretary and Mr. Skubal were the dream team.

I attended a Christian school in South Chicago Heights for kindergarten to make sure I did not have to be penalized by sitting an entire school year out due to the birth date rule. If you were not 5 years old by September 1 entering as a kindergartner, you had to wait until that following school year. So unfortunate! Thank God my mom provided a way for me to stay ahead of the game.

I made a few good friends in kindergarten and grammar school. I thought I had an exclusive relationship with this one boy. My

mom and his mom worked together. We attended the Christian school together. Being that young there was always a birthday party invitation or someone's mom was bringing in cupcakes to celebrate a birthday. Well, this boy that I had a crush on and the feeling was mutual invited me to Red Lobster for his birthday celebration. Are you reading this? Feelings at five years old? Get out of here!

I know my mom was strict but she allowed me to enjoy my childhood with some limits. I get all dolled up to go to Red Lobster which was a great deal being so young and considered upscale to me as well. I use to love those cheddar biscuits. To my dismay, when we arrive I realized he invited all the girls he had a crush on. Boys are just no good...Ha!

I don't recall too much happening in the first grade other than the teacher being so sweet and soft spoken but I do recall making glue handprints in the second grade. Do you remember this? You would peel the glue of your hands in hopes of the perfect peel-off. My second grade teacher used to my pull my pig tails when she did not think I was responding fast enough to her requests. My mother thought she was the best teacher alive. That's because the teacher used to buy Avon from my mother every pay period. Boy! I tell you....

What I recalled in third grade was being excited to be a student of Ms. Perna but she so happened to be out on maternity leave the majority of my third grade year. The substitute was an older black lady who did not play any games. I quickly learned that I could not even snicker in her class. The one time I messed up and let my laughter overpower my ability to show discipline, the substitute teacher made me grab the old school encyclopedias and hold two  of them in each hand with one foot raised off the ground. I never had good balance...until I accepted God wholeheartedly into my life.

In grammar school, I first realized my hands would sweat profusely. I had no control over this issue and complained to my parents how it affected my school work. My paper would roll up around the edges because the paper was soaking wet from my sweaty hands. My parents took me to the doctor regarding this concern. The doctor only suggestion was to cut the sweat glands out of my hands. Now that everything is technology-driven, I wonder what options I have now. My hands still sweat profusely. Was it anxiety? I started to pick up a little weight…okay…a lot of weight and I wore these larger than life glasses that resembled magnifying glasses. To this day, my mom says they came from Sears. I don't know about all that!

This is where times became a little trying in school because for one while, this young man was known as a bully. Just looking at him made my hands drip sweat and my knees buckle. He even gave some of the teachers a hard time and at this particular time that was unheard of. I was wondering if he knew that Mr. Skubal was the principal/reinforcer. Was I in another world or something? Someone explain this to me, please. One day, I cracked a joke in class and he laughed. That was my moment to capitalize and make sure I kept the jokes going. I went from being bullied to being the one bullying others. I became the class clown on the low. I wasn't

disruptive to the point I was addressed because the teachers would not even believe it if the students said it was me causing friction while their heads were turned. I became a protégé of my youngest brother. I was an instigator and number one roaster. Roasting meant you were involved in a laugh session putting another person on blast or fronting them. It always started off with, "get yo' big". If the sentence did not start off like this you probably got muffed; which means someone pushed your head enough to make you move.

When it was time to go out for recess I had become the girl my brothers used to roughen up to make sure I did not take no stuff off of anyone. The timing was right. I would wrestle with the boys, play basketball, and even tackle some not because I was being fast but because I did not have to compete or be concerned with how my hair looked. This kept the boys from talking about me and had some of the girls scared or befriended me because they would rather have me as a friend than an enemy.

I made some lasting relationships and have been able to keep in touch with quite a few along the way. Some we have lost to violence and drugs but they will always remain a part of our lives. There was a time when my father was running for office as an elected official. He brought flyers to be distributed around the school. I don't know if I was embarrassed or proud; maybe a combination of both. Here it is where those who knew me  along with my school principal, knew very little about this man who pops up as my father. Many knew he existed but only saw my mother and brothers caring for me before and after school.

I look back and understand the love daughters have for their father and when that bond is broken voluntarily or involuntarily, can take a toll on the decisions she make throughout her life. No excuses. I am stating my truth. He was something else. He saw an opportunity and jumped right on board. The opportunities may have been seen as being far-fetched but it did not matter to him, none whatsoever. He was a go-getter. He seemed fearless yet, realized he feared more than what we were able to comprehend.

When children come from different walks of life and are blended and bonded together while in school, children can feel pressured. There was this sixth-grader who had a chest, hips, and even began her period. We all sat at lunch together exchanging stories as if we were in a hair salon on a Saturday morning. You know the talk was good then. Some were telling their truths as a replica of their mother or a woman in their life who talks just like what the girls were mimicking. One of the girls go on to tell us that she needed to go to the bathroom and change her pad. What? Not only did Ms. Naïve (me) not understand what was going on but I was pretty confident that this should not have been a conversation to openly talk about. She takes out this little packaged square and proceed to go to the bathroom. Excuse me! I was too outdone. I had to pull my compadre to the side and ask what was really going on. For the next few weeks in lunch the discussions that were happening played a major part in how I carried myself and how I associate with people. These girls had a little girl praying harder than I had ever prayed before.

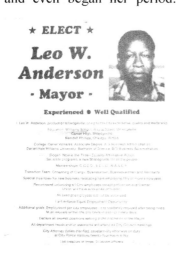

★ ELECT ★

Leo W. Anderson

- Mayor -

Experienced ● Well Qualified

Girls were talking about who was liking and kissing who, who they were going to beat up for looking at them the wrong way, and who ain't a part of the clique anymore because she doing too much. This was too petty but I was trying to find my way.

I did not want to hang with the boys anymore because it just did not feel right. Some of the girls were too fast and the other weren't fast enough....lame.

But guess what. I was a cool lame and that was alright with me...so I thought. Fifth and sixth grade, I was in the gifted program; competing in spelling bees and math competitions. Science was not my subject at all. I stayed at the top of the class and then it was time to transition to middle school.

Picture day used to be fun because I had the chance to dress up and get my hair pressed like I was getting ready for church on an early Sunday morning. Everyone did not get the chance to

 see me all dolled up. I thought I was doing it big. Some of the pictures I was struck though. My brothers had to pull my hair together for a few of those pictures because mom was running late from work or worked a double shift. My middle brother was trying to cut one of those hair balls out of my hair and mistakenly cut an entire braid. Boy what's wrong with you? You got me out here bad.

I attended Gwendolyn Brooks Junior High School in Harvey, IL for 7th and 8th grade. Those were the longest two years of my life. I dealt with so many emotions that I was relieved to get to high school. Then that was another battle. My mother became a little more lenient when I got to middle school because a sister could not even cross the street to play. Some of my so-called friends were so bogus that when we disagreed on something, they would cross the street and play. Oh well!

The great thing that happened was that I was selected to attend Governors State University summer of '93 and '94 for a money matters gifted program. I always said I was going back to that place for college. I did not know I was going to experience as many hardships as I did but I made it back there July 2010.

You have to learn to embrace who you are. You won't be young all your life and there will be a time when you'll have to put your big girl panties on and toughen up. Don't wear your feelings on your sleeve and don't expect others to hold your hand. Trust God and never doubt Him. He will never leave you nor forsake you. There will be times when you question your purpose. Why fit in when you were made to stand out? When you attempt to walk a path of your own choosing you become confused and desperate for guidance which turns into vulnerability if unattended for a prolonged period of time.

We always hear people talk about thinking outside the box when we need to focus more on throwing the box away.

I knew I belonged to God way before I even understood the reason as to why. All of the challenges of trying to fit in with people during a time where I had no clue who I was or why I felt the way I did made it impossible for me to run from God the rest of my life. I had to surrender but I kept running from the calling.

"Come to me, all you who are weary and burdened, and I will give you rest. Take my yoke upon you and learn from me, for I am gentle and humble in heart, and you will find rest for your souls. 30 For my yoke is easy and my burden is light."
~ Matthew 11:28-30

Chapter Six

16320 S. Carse Avenue

Excuses are monuments of nothingness. They build bridges to nowhere. Those of us who use these tools of incompetence, seldom become anything but nothing at all. ~ Unknown

Home sweet home.....my mother still lives here to this day. I remember when she first showed interest in purchasing this house even though I had no clue this was going to be our permanent home without my father. When we came to this house, there was no grass just mud along with some structural construction under way. As soon as we entered the house that was off-white brick with navy blue fixtures, I knew I wanted the first bedroom. There were a total of three bedrooms and the family (my mother, three brothers, and me) have all reunited. So, let me get this right, you mean to tell me we have to fit five people into a three bedroom ranch-style home with no basement and only one bathroom???

When you have to make life decisions, you are not concerned with the luxuries as long as you are safe and out of harm's way. If I'd only known some of the hell my mother and brothers went through.

I was excited to be moving into our new home. I sat my jacket on the stove to check out the rest of the house. There weren't any counters yet. They were installing them prior to us moving in. My jacket caught fire. We put that little flame out quick. That just goes to show you

how excited I was for my entire family to be back together

again. But there was only one discrepancy to this story. My dad was not coming.

I thought they had settled their differences and hoped for the best. The best to me meant being selfish to request my family to be under one roof again like before. I did not understand then but I understand now. Honestly, I feel for my family because they never sought the healing needed to seek closure. I know he was my father and there are speculations of bias  because of our relationship differing from others, but the truth remains.

If you have ever endured pain from a past hurt, seek God first and it doesn't hurt to seek professional help. Generally speaking, we do not like seeking help. We think the idea of doing so is weak and abnormal. What we fail to realize is that  those deep-rooted hurts from our past currently dwells in our lives. Some of the decisions we make are based on what we experienced and if those decisions are made out of misery, you will never reach a place of healing.

If you can kill the negativity in your mind, you can kill it in your life! Believe that! Receive it! The mind is a terrible thing to waste......United Negro College Fund (UNCF)

While my mother and brothers strategically planned to move and leave my father for good, my mom sent me to my Aunt Bea's home. Having the big mouth I had, my mother could not chance my dad knowing what was going on. Once they moved in, I was welcomed to a home where my mother and brothers worked together to care for my well-being. My brothers took turns throughout the week to babysit which included help with homework when needed, feeding me, and supervising my nightly routine to get ready for bed.

Mind you, the conscious decision my mother made to finally live in peace was one of the most remarkable decisions I ever  witnessed her make. It meant great sacrifice but the she began to reap what she had sowed for so long. The struggle was real yet we lived in harmony. Yeah, there were three young men living under her roof who all experienced their "I'm too grown for this" moments but they each fell in line or left the nest to experience life from a different perspective.

Love - love everything about you from your hair or the lack thereof to your unique smile. Always walk with your head held high with proper structure. Fall so deep in love with yourself so you'll know and expect to be treated right.

Speaking on love, I am reminded of God's Word regarding the nine fruits of the Holy Spirit: "But the fruit of the Spirit is love, joy, peace, longsuffering, kindness, goodness, faithfulness, gentleness, self-control." (Galatians 5:22)

Do you operate in all nine fruits? If not, why?

My mother recently announced to me that everyone respects her but me. Complete strangers respect her more than I do. Now while I do not agree with her, I will say that we do have an odd relationship. What she may fail to realize is that I had lived in resentment for years and took close to two decades to ask God for forgiveness. I was a rebel. If my mother said yes, I said no and vice versa. I will admit that the loving and God-fearing child she birthed and raised for the first 14 years of my life had become one who worshipped foolishness. I thrived off of ignorance yet failed to realize the damage it caused me. Yes, I hurt my mother but I hurt me more. I lost me to prove a point. I was a rebel with no cause.

Predestined
The desire to serve something greater than you
Say yes to destiny – destiny draws you
Do you know your purpose?
For so long, I searched for love....a love I could not find.
That love led to abuse, depression, and isolation. That wasn't love now was it?

When I gave it all to God my life changed.

I had to learn that I cannot live for my mother. My mother is not my God. She is a spiritual woman who I admire for her faith but she is still human and has feelings just like me. She faced many challenges just like me. I could not continue living my life trying to make up for past hurts and pains. I cannot help that when you look at this young, Black female you see a  strong resemblance of my father. I am not my father. I loved him with no conditions and even in his absence, I chose to love him. The irony of this entire situation is that the many sacrifices my mother made were appreciated later in life but the one who was absent received my loyalty.

We have to remember that it is not what you do for people that  gain their loyalty and faithfulness it is how you made them feel when in your presence. If I leave a lasting impression in one moment, that moment speaks volumes in your life. Father-daughter relationships are very important. They shape the fabric of standards for her whether it teaches her what not to do or what not to accept. Believe me. I am a mother of four young ladies and one male and the absence of their biological fathers has been detrimental to our lives. Now, their stepfather is dynamic but he does not play the damsel in distress role with any one of them because his philosophy is that your past or the absence of someone significant cannot define your being. You have to make a conscious effort to live a meaningful life regardless of the circumstances. Hell...if that was the case I should have been dead by now.

Even then when people are loyal and faithful there will be times where they may disappoint. Baby...this is what we call life! Are you up for the challenge? We cannot possibly live our entire existence thinking the sun shines and sets on our back ends. Nope. Don't do it.

Lord, help me to overcome my fears by filling my mind with positive thoughts and my life with positive actions. This was my prayer prior to placing all the broken fragments together to write this piece of inspiration. My favorite quote is, "God is." God is (you fill in the blank). For me, God is everything!

"My desire is to be a life advocate; having experienced many life situations. Still I stand." ~ SJ

Oh! The house parties that commenced while my mother was hustling working the night shift. My brothers had the house juking from the moment my mother's car was no longer visible on Carse Avenue. The hood rats, the fellas, the alcohol, spades, and shooting dice was a nightly ritual until mama shut

it ALL THE WAY DOWN! Thank God no one was ever hurt during the recklessness. No wonder why I was so confused. Moms teaching me to love the Lord with all my heart while two of my three brothers ran a whore house by night. Now they would tell me to go into my room and watch TV until I would fall asleep but you already know Nosey Rosey had to see what was happening around these parts.

I was not even allowed to play across the street. I had to come in the house when the street lights came on. Ha! Ha! Ha! Did anyone else have to come in the house when the street lights came on? I should've just broken all the street lights on Carse. Just kidding! I still keep in touch with most of my childhood friends thanks to Facebook.

My mother can discern just about anything. She may have not known the full details of what all occurred, but she was always on point with whatever details she had. My brothers thought I was a snitch. Snitches get stitches or in my case my brothers would lock me in the room with the red light on while Thriller by Michael Jackson played in the background. That video and song terrified me. Sibling love. While we are on the subject of snitching, what's the deal? I wished more people exercised a level of maturity to understand the need to be transparent in specific situations. No, We'd rather keep a secret that hinders the lives of others. I understand fully that there are situations that prevent people from coming forward with details of what occurred due to fear but something has to give.

This is the home I transitioned from, the angel to the enemy.

I watched my mother struggle with medical challenges while working for a state mental health facility night after night. When she left that position, she studied to become a real estate agent. She sold some of the best homes in the south suburban Cook County area. When the homes were not selling like hot cakes, my mother's faith and prayer life kept her encouraged. I do not know how she did it.

My brothers were leaving home and starting their own journeys which left the two of us to rely on each other. She was my

 everything and I was a replica of her. I allowed the enemy to tear us apart because as we (there is a word missing here) our struggle grew more and more evident; I could not understand how she could remain so faithful to God in the midst of our storm. Her pride did not allow us to ask for help. But, I watched several individuals over a period of time, walk up to her during church service and bless her with a love token. She was a faithful tither and no matter what financial issues we faced in the home, she continued to press her way to our church home.

Sunday, we were in church all day; Sunday School, regular service, dinner (at Glady's which was one of my mother's first jobs as a short order cook migrating from Drew, Mississippi),  and Young People Willing Workers (YPWW) night service. To add to the long, exhausting day, my mother volunteered to bring the juice and donuts for Sunday School participants, which meant we would be the first ones to church along with the faithful deacon. If that was not enough, we would drop my aunt off at her home after night service that led to hours of sitting in the car waiting on someone to walk her into her high rise building on 43rd and Federal; Robert Taylor Homes.

For one, while, I envied the relationship my mother had with her oldest sister because I felt I was in competition for my mother's attention. I shared her with everyone. If she was not consumed by her spiritual life, she sought to care for others; especially her oldest sister. Then I began to live as an adult and found that if no one else cared then why not YOU! Now, I am pretty sure that my babies feel the same way about me to a certain extent. Damn!

This is the home I transitioned from the angel to the enemy.

The older I got and the stronger the need to fit in with other peers as I entered high school, I began to rebel. If she said yes, I made it my life's mission to say no. Who the ^&*$ did I think I was. Once my brothers got a whiff of my ways, they would attempt to chastise me and I rebelled against them as well. Where the hell were you when mama and I had to share a pack of noodles for dinner? Where were you when the bill collectors continuously called until one night my mama told me to just let them hold? The bill collector held that phone for over an hour waiting on my mama, LOL! Where were you when I thought it was normal for all the mail to be pink once you opened the envelope?

They were living their life like they were supposed to. My  problem was that for all of my life, my mother and brothers sheltered me from harm and I never knew what the struggle was because they protected me. They spoiled me and made sure I did not want for anything. So when the time of struggle crept upon us I had no clue as to what in 'Sam Hill' was going on. I could not comprehend going from sugar to s#$%.

I had to jump ship because my selfishness and vain ways got the best of me. I turned my back on my mama during the most crucial times of our lives. We were supposed to be there for one another even if there was a sense of resentment. She sacrificed everything for my well-being and my ungrateful a$% could not see past the vanity.

Mama, please forgive me.

This is the home I transitioned from the angel to the enemy.

I was about eight or nine years old when I wanted to play with the next door neighbor's kids. Let my mama tell it they were Bay-Bay's kids. This lady had about five or six children running around 24/7. She told me I needed to come in the house for a nap. What? Where they do that at? This was one of the first instances of showing out and talking back. I put my hands on my hips and told her I did not want to take a nap. I wanted to play with the next door neighbor's kids. I then went on to tell her that we were doing fine when we were with my daddy and she messed it all up. That sister ran up behind me so quick that I did not know what happened to me. I was dazed. When I managed to get away, I ran into the bedroom and jumped out of the window to get outside.

My next door neighbor picked me up off the driveway pavement and carried me to the front door. Was I crazy? Am I crazy still? I complained of a few aches. Moms took me to the hospital to get checked out. I was alright but of course the speculation was that my mama whipped me. She let the hospital officials know exactly just that. The next day, someone from the Department of Children and Family Services (DCFS) called to question my mama. She let them have it and we never heard from them again.

See the turmoil disobedient children put their parents through? Believe me, I have paid a hefty bill for all of my shenanigans.

I think I should have named the book 16320 because all of my life occurrences happened here and this is where I retreated for

comfort. Look at me, just a big baby running to her mama. I honestly believe this was my issue. As long as my mama had an open door policy I took advantage thinking she will always be available to me. I am thankful she is still here on this earth but I had to learn to stop running to mama and to run to the Thrown of Grace. I had to seek God for myself. I cannot go to my mama to solve my problems. Now, I go to my war room. If you have not seen this movie, War Room you are missing out on something great. War Room inspired me to create my very own war room where I can have peace to talk to the Lord, pray, and write my thoughts. I even placed my 2016 gratitude jar and my loose change box in my war room because I need to write the blessings on paper every day and our finances need to be blessed as well.

My three oldest children and my youngest were born at my mama's home. My fourth child was born while attempting to live an independent life as a wife and mother.

My oldest daughter had just celebrated her first birthday with all of our family and friends. It was one of those hood birthday parties. More adults than children. Chicken wings, hot dogs, kool-aid and pop. Oh! Ice cream and cake too! My mother pleaded with me to stay in the house that night but I wanted to hang with my friends. I should've listened. This was my first of many "documented" run-ins with the police. As soon as I stepped out the door there was drama waiting. Two of my neighbors were arguing about a deal that went wrong. I am trying to be the peacemaker. Failed. The police arrive on the scene and tells everyone to get out the street and go indoors. I got out of the street and onto the sidewalk. I talked a little trash. The police left. Of course they had to return because the situation between the neighbors was out of control.

How did I get in the mix of it all? I was the one who called the police because I wanted our one block to remain peaceful unless I was the one causing the friction, lol. One of the officers approached me and was yelling so loud, I blanked out. I'm screaming to the top of my lungs, "WHO YOU TALKING TO LIKE THAT?" We are going back and forth and no other officer is intervening. It's quite funny to them. The officer tells me, "I should whip you like your daddy should've!" The girl with the daddy issues completely lost her damn mind. Now, the other officers come along and tell my one girlfriend to take me into the house (my BFFs house). The moment she pushes me down the sidewalk, the officer I was feuding with come and hits her with his stick. He then takes his stick and wedges it between the screen and wooden door. He enters the home to fight with me. We are fighting! I am laying haymakers, body slamming him, and he is taking it all. The other officers are laughing until they felt it was getting too out of hand. All along my BFF mother is trying to resolve the issue but they think she is a young chick like us. They haul me and my friend who was trying to push me into the house to lock-up. I could not believe it.

One of the girls from the notorious family known for setting s$%^ off was in the cell next to us singing spirituals. That was the only funny thing about the entire night. Oh! That and when I laid my head on my girlfriend's lap to go to sleep. My middle brother's best friend was on the police force at that time too! He came to my rescue that night. I had to appear before a judge and received community service. The officer was reprimanded as well. Wow! I should've listened to my mom.

If I could offer a piece of advice right now, raise your children.

As much as I would love for ladies and gentlemen to have children after marriage and have stability, the world does not work like that. Do not use the excuse of being a teen parent to allow others to raise your children because it will come back to bite you in the a$$. Whatever sexual act/position took place to conceive a child that child is your responsibility. You cannot claim to be grown when in actuality you solely rely on someone else to care for you and your seed. Assistance is one thing but when someone else plays more of a role in your child's life, we all have a problem. This is the mistake I made. Staying under someone else's roof causes conflict because your parenting skills may be totally different than theirs. The way you operate is different. Your schedule is different.

I am tired of hearing the constant reminders of what someone did back in my hay day when I had no clue of what being a mother was. I will admit my faults. I wanted to run the streets even with two I was responsible for. I  wanted to chase behind foolishness. I am so glad the Lord stepped in and ordered my steps. To each his/her own but I am so glad God forgave me and gave me another chance. Others hold you to your past or only want you to progress to a level of their liking. Be careful of these types of people. As long as God is pleased, I cannot be held to what others deem suitable for me.

The world is ever changing but He remains the same. People will disappoint you and you will disappoint them but God is a forgiving God who will give you a clean slate. We're always tripping over what we did or what we did not do, yet God has kept it moving. What are you waiting on? Why haven't you moved on? Baby, forgive yourself.

He Saved Me from Myself

My ability to show concern for others prevented me from loving myself

While I focused on the needs of others, I placed mine on the shelf

I said, "I'll have time to handle my own needs when I completed other plans

Yet the will of God comes after man's
I thought I was on the straight and narrow and doing the very best that I could
Yet here I am again realizing that I am not doing the work that I should
He said, "trust me, I'll give you rest"
But here I am again driving my own quest
How did I expect to make it, how did I survive?
How do I learn to live ad make my spirit come alive?
I don't challenge my negative beliefs; I continue to live in the past
I endure the pain of what I used to be, although I want my legacy to last
I'm struggling to heal; I'm hurt from some of the difficult situations
My body is weak. My spirit suffers from those masculine temptations
I've always wanted to be a living testimony but didn't know that this road would be quite like this
At times I feel like a complete failure as if my life is a hit or miss
My times have been overwhelming even through times where I've tried to end it all
Because the world I chose to live in, I was unclear for when He would call
My temple has been abused, assaulted, and damaged
As I write this passage, I can see why my life is unmanaged
I'll admit that I have lost total control of my life
Failing to gain a sense of a nurturer as a mom or wife
Have you ever given so much of yourself that you have nothing left for self?

Have you ever cried at the drop of a dime and asked God to save you from yourself?
Being able to visually see what needs to be done; guided by Him
To stop and listen even when the lights are dim
Here I am several years later thanking God for rescuing me
He forgave me and gave me a clean slate so I can be what He requires me to be

Chapter Seven

17101 S. PARK AVENUE

Oh! The joy of being a freshman at Thornwood High School, where the prestige met the 'hood. We lived in the first ward of Harvey where the school boundaries were complex and still is if you ask me. While some went to Thornton others went to Thornwood for high school. The unfortunate part of it all was that many of the faces you saw every day for the last 9 to 10 years faded away because we were split between two schools.

My student ID number was 340370. One of my best friend's student ID number was 340371. The similarity caused us a lot of issues. Well, it caused me a lot of issues.

My freshman year was pretty smooth. I was known for being the goofiest girl who cracked jokes 24/7. Those big a$$ glasses had to go and I needed an upgrade on wardrobe. Yeah, that all came along in the latter part of my freshman or sophomore year of high school and I paid a hefty price to look a certain way. Mind you, I still had to be in the house by the time the street lights came on. My mother would stand on the front porch and yell my name to the top of her lungs, "SHA-KNEE-QWA!" Come on now, really?

I would get on the bus and the one boy who set my hair on fire when we were in grade school would mimic the way my mother would yell my name. Don't do me boo. It was all good because I had a master plan. Just give me some time.

I made good grades and never caused any havoc. Everything was easy breezy. My homeroom teacher, Mr. Torrance could do 100 push-ups in less than a minute. Other students would come in the classroom in the mornings to see him do his thang.

After the third time seeing him do these push-ups, I was no longer impressed. For real!

My homeroom classmates were not rowdy whatsoever. Everyone was pretty laid back. We cracked our jokes from time-to-time but there were never any detrimental issues. I can recall running through the hallways all the time and just being the average freshman during that particular era.

You know that high school life brings different people in a new environment meant you started to create a new life. Your clique changed.

One clique I was down for during my high school years was The Roaches. Yes. The Roaches. The Roaches consisted of three key members; me included and four other individuals; two older and two younger. If I can recall, we started calling ourselves roaches summer '95 but I may be off by a year. What I do remember is that we hung tight. When you saw one, you saw us all. Do you remember the movie, Joe's Apartments (1996)? Well our "gang" (which we weren't) was heavily inspired by this movie. We weren't afraid to say we were roaches once the movie highlighted these hilarious roaches as characters.

The point was that the majority of us had darker complexions and refused to come outside during the day. I guess I had a complex. I was heavier than everyone else and one of the darker girls in the clique.

We were too busy listening to TuPac …well I was too busy listening to raps like TuPac's, "I Ain't Mad at Cha or Warren G's, "Regulate" during the day and rewinding the tape to hear the songs over and over in order to write the lyrics. Oh! Crucial Conflict's song, "Hay" was my joint too! We would be at the corner house all day and night doing our homework (if any) and playing Monopoly. This was my "I am going to be fast" house; my second home. Let me not forget....I used to love the group, Jodeci. Let me quit playing, I still love Jodeci.

My mama and I were piss poor. Our dinner consisted of sharing a pack of Ramen noodles and an ice cold water. We only had one ice tray so that glass of ice water was like gold. Man, when I say times were hard that's what I mean. This is one of the reasons why I chose the path I did in order to make sure I was able to enjoy the luxuries.

The Roaches would go to the local food joint, PJ's up the street to eat. I could not afford it but would ask for a few dollars every once in a while. This one particular time, I went in the house after school while my girls stood on the front porch. I asked my mama for a couple of dollars so I could eat at PJ's

with my girls. She yelled, "You better go in there and eat them noodles and I don't want to hear your fat lip!" I stared at her for a long minute in disbelief because she was loud. Too loud. I go back outside and before I could give an excuse, my girls mimicked my mama by repeating what she had just yelled at me. Embarrassing!

They looked out for me though. We all had a great bond and looked out for one another.

So I am entering my sophomore year of high school and I am starting to feel this rebellious spirit. I was 14 on the cusp of being 15 in a few months. I turned 15 on November 22, 1995 and had sex for the very first time right after that; Christmas 1995. I talk about this later on during this journey. Anyway, it was horrible but now I think I'm on something. Not! It was bunk. It was the worst.

But, I gradually became the girl I never wanted to be. I was supposed to be this God-fearing young lady who wanted to be used as a vessel. Here I am at the age of 35 as of November 22, 2015, and I am just making my way back. I am so glad God forgives. Even at some of my lowest points.

The Roaches started hanging with the Black Disciples (BDs) across Halsted (one block east of Halsted to be exact) getting into all types of trouble. Although I never had sex with any of them or even the one I called my boyfriend at the time, we were up to no good at that particular time. He wanted me to do things I was good at talking about but I was not putting in any action. You want me to put my mouth where? You want me to bend over and do what exactly?

Hell, after my first and only experience I knew I was cool on all that. I gave up my precious goods by default. You'll see what I am talking about in another chapter. I promise. Shawty can't go out like that....nope.

One night in February '96, I am with my Roaches kicking it with the BDs and as we are crossing Halsted we notice a patch of ice right by the alleyway. We laughed and reminded ourselves that we need to be careful when we are headed back. My mother always told me to take the long (street route) to the corner store or anywhere else I traveled. She told me to stay out of the alleys. Don't nothing good happens in those alleys.

I was too hard-headed. But they say a hard head makes a soft bottom or hard ankle in my case. One of my BFFs and I had a 9pm curfew that we never wanted anyone to know so we always made excuses that we were sleepy or had homework to finish. All lies...lies I tell ya! Ha!

We are crossing Halsted in a hurry to get home and make 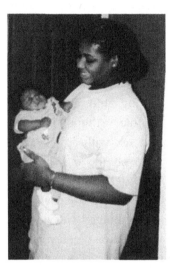 curfew. We are running like we are running for our lives. The next thing you know, my BFF and I both fall on the ice we had forgotten about in a hurry to make curfew. My BFF was able to get right up. I was not. I later learned that black ice was the worst ice to come across because it's deceiving in appearance. Later down the line, Mrs. Black Ice became my personal nick name because that was the essence of who I had become.

When I tried to get up I realized my ankle felt real light.

The majority of my left ankle had detached from my leg. I was so in shock that I could not even gather one tear. My BFF ran for help while I was told to stay put. What she did not know was that the homeless and drunks from the abandoned car wash which is now Dunkin' Donuts were coming to get me. I didn't know if they were coming to help, steal, or rape me and I was not going to continue lying there to find out. I hauled a$$. I limped and crawled until I reached my BFFs backyard. Her mother's friend came to assist her by carrying me into their home. That was a fiasco too! There was a trail of broken ligaments from where I fell to her backyard.

My BFFs mother called my mom and told her that she needed to get over to their home ASAP. I instantly began to wail when my mother walked in. I was more afraid of facing her than I was of the possibility of losing my ankle. We gently got me into my mother's car and because we had no insurance, she drove to Provident Hospital, a county hospital for us poor folks. Provident Hospital is on 51st street. We lived on 163rd. Can you imagine this long dreadful drive? My BFF and her family trailed us. I could feel every pothole and bump in the road. I moaned and cringed every few seconds. By the time we reached the hospital, my ankle had swollen to quadruple the size of my right ankle.

We were in the waiting area of the emergency room forever. I watched an older gentlemen flick boogers across the room. He reminded me of the character, Anton from the TV show, In Living Color. People of all walks of life with different medical issues crowded the emergency room. Finally, the clerk called my name and I went straight to the back for medical attention. We get to the back and the guy is trying to reset my ankle in order to put me in a soft cast. The ankle was so sensitive to touch and swollen that they had to cut my brand new Guess jeans and my left Nike gym shoe that my youngest brother and wife had just bought me. In all of my agony I asked if they could do something different as opposed to cutting my gear. Nope! They had to cut it.

They finally realized that this was an issue bigger than they could handle. We were notified that I would have to be transferred to Cook County Hospital in order to receive the proper medical attention needed. My mother told my BFF and her family that I was being transferred and that their support was appreciated. They left and went back home. As the ambulance transferred me from Provident to Cook County

Hospital, my mother trailed right behind us. Later in my journey, my mother shared with me that God reminded her to be grateful through this horrific trial. He gave her a peace when He brought to her attention that she could have been following a hearse instead of an ambulance.

The doctors informed us that if I had hit my head the way I damaged my ankle, I would have died. But the God I no longer served to protect me anyway. The medical staff immediately relieved me of my pain by injecting me with Stadol. I was off my rocker. I saw clouds. I was floating. I was laughing uncontrollably. I had no control. That was the best high ever or so I thought. In my 30s I experienced an ultimate high when I accepted Jesus as my Lord and Savior. Now that is the best high!

This was worse than I thought. I shared a room with a young child who had lost their right leg. I was instantly reminded to

be grateful. The cries. The moans. That cold and wet basement feeling I strongly despised consumed me. I felt like I was in the psych ward. I cried until there were no more tears.

The next morning I was prepped for surgery. The damage was so severe that a specialist from across the country had to fly in to perform the surgery. The results were two metal plates, bolts, and screws. I was told I would walk with a limp for the rest of my life. They advised that I would have to carry my medical documents when entering establishments with metal detectors, and that it would take a prolonged period of time to learn how to walk again.

The road to recovery was tiresome. I went to physical therapy. I managed to do just enough to be released. But, I could not return to school for several weeks. My mother enrolled me into home school and my instructors came to my home throughout the week. I made straight A's the entire time I was enrolled as a home school student. Wow! I had to put this all on paper to understand the unconditional love my mother has for me even through my craziness.

My rebellion caused her heartache, many inconveniences, unneeded stress, and anxiety. This is ridiculous. Because I was sleep during surgery, I had no idea what the incision looked like and neither did my mom.

Looking

Love,- where have you've been, because it seems
as if you don't like coming around me,
and when I get a hold to it, it seems as if
your not wanting to be near. Why everyone
says that]aunt you, but when it comes
to me, I'm still looking. One day I'll be
lucky just to have you nearby, I wrote
this letter thinking maybe if I try to
explain my situation, you'll solve
this problem. Please consider me as
a person looking for love and not a
person desperate for love. cause long
as I live being desperate will never be
in me.
                            Love Always,
                                 Wanting Love.

When I returned to the doctor's office for my follow-up appointment to have my staples removed, we had our first look at what was hiding underneath my cast. Oh! My oldest brother decked my cast out. I wish he knew how much of a great detailed and creative artist he is. My leg was so small I was thinking to ask the doctor to cast my stomach. Ha! As they are taking the cast off, me and my mom are as nervous as can be. The incision was close to 5 inches long. What! Fam, ya did not tell me all of this. What am I supposed to do with a 5-inch scar? Cocoa butter or fade cream can't do anything for this.

I cried uncontrollably. I got over it when I imagined death or an even more crippling disability. The thing about high school was that when you went missing from the scene for more than three days, the streets (hallways) got to talking. Some thought I ran away. If that was the case, why didn't you come looking for me? Some thought I had a baby. Nope. Not yet! They jinxed me, lol. I jinxed myself! The recovery wasn't too bad and I was ready to go back to school.

My mother and I had a great support system while I was recovering. The saints from the church were checking on us. My friends would stop by to let me know what was going on at school. The Roaches were always around. Those were my peeps. Let me stop here to explain how something so simple and silly turned into chaos.

Because we formed our own clique, some other neighborhood girls formed one too. We fought every day. We fought on the bus. We tortured them. They tortured us. It was all senseless. The thing was, The Roaches had formed a strong union and we were all from the same neighborhood while some of the girls from the other clique were family to some of the girls who were apart of the rival clique. The other part is that we were more diverse in age. Two were in junior high school. Three of us were in high school. Two were adults with small children.

I know it sound so childish and innocent but that's who we were; goofy a$$ girls. We had a handshake. We wore certain colors. We would start walking by putting our left foot first.

Too much. It was like a wild fire because this was supposed to be a neighborhood thing. We would get to school and others start recognizing us as The Roaches. We had our little candy store gig popping off at my locker.

My locker had become the one stop shop for all your candy and school supply needs. We were innocent hustlers and we had minimal issues until I got called to the dean office. My dean asks me if I was a gang leader. What? C'mon now. You know me better than that, sir. I might be a part of a clique but I definitely ain't in no gang and you better not call my mama with this foolishness. He pulls out the gang list for our school and sure as boo-boo stank, our clique is listed along with my name as the leader.

He then goes on to inform me that our clique was a front for the Sisters of the Struggle. Man, look. I ain't about to sit here and be pressured into agreeing with your opinion of what we are and what we stand for. I'm just not. That blows over. But the real issues were seeing guys that grew up together feud because some are Vice Lords, a couple are Gangster Disciples (GDs), some are Black Stone, etc. So you have known this guy for 15 plus years and now neither of you can be friends or even cordial because your star has one more/one less point than the other? Really?

This gang banging foolishness is ridiculous. I am going to befriend whoever I want and I am going to certain neighborhoods without fear of being attacked. If I don't fool with you, it has nothing to do with your gang affiliation.

I wasn't the hardest thing alive neither. I was jumped by seven or eight girls because one of their own thought I had a full relationship with one of the guys from the neighborhood who happened to be her child's father (baby daddy). I got a few licks in but they got up with my glamour. I cracked my jokes since I knew the outcome wasn't going to work in my favor. I got up and wiped the dirt of my shoulder like Jay-Z said in his song.

With everything I thought I had going on outside of school I still I had to go to church. When I turned 15, I personally told the Lord that He and I were through. I had given him 15 good years of my life and now it's time for me to get out and about. To satisfy my mom since I wanted to be with my BFF, I started going to church with her and her family. Just take a wild guess why I was so interested in going to church with my BFF? If you said the Lord, just stop reading now. Truth was…I was boy crazy.

I was into this dude who was not from the neighborhood, wasn't trying to get my used goods (so I thought), went to church, seemed level-headed, and was decent looking. The problem was that I learned he went to the same high school as me. And I don't want to deal with other chicks whatsoever; especially at school. I learned early on that the best accessory a man can have been a woman by his side. Now, I may have been a teen but when you recognize something, whether it's personal or something you observe, truth is truth.

A man can be single and no one cares but the moment he starts seeing someone, the women (girls) start flocking. I promise you, I wasn't lady-like whatsoever. I would push my tongue down his throat in front of the church. My BFF's mother was so soft spoken and the sweetest woman I ever met, but she let me have it when she saw me acting like a lil' hood rat. I couldn't help myself. He was a really sweet guy. My mind's telling me no but my body… (insert R. Kelly's Bump-n-Grind music). I was a big tease though. I would only go so far. I think what ended our relationship (one of the ones my mama knew about and had approved) was when he wanted to visit my church. Awh! Here we go. He came to our home on a Mother's Day and brought my mama some roses. Hold up. What about me? That was the first indication that we were going to wrap this here relationship up. We all ride to church together. He's almost too polite. That was the second indication that we was about to be through. Oh! I am not the "three strikes you're out" type of gal (not then at least), I was done. Whatever feels you got was over. I never gave him my used goods neither. Good!

Well, I am a little older and have physically changed. My "sweet 16" came and went. My mother and sister-in law had planned to celebrate my 16th birthday, but my fast tail wanted to run the streets. Birthday cake? Nah! I'm cool on that. Me and my BFFs went to our nail technician who lived right across the street from the BDs. I stayed in trouble with them girls. But because my mother was so strict, I could not figure out a way to maneuver without getting caught up in my mess.

I entered my junior year of high school at 15 turning 16 that November. The glasses were gone. I got a perm. My hair is laid. I'm starting to get my nails done. I had lost some weight. I had titties! I had a little booty and I was feeling myself. When I first started trying to hang tough like I was a hood chick I was 14. I saw this dude who was driving these nice cars with sounds and rims. During this time, I was wearing glitter lip gloss and body lotion. Glitter was everywhere. Literally, everywhere.

I even went through a gothic stage where I wore all black clothing, black lipstick, and black nail polish. I wanted everyone to think I was intimidating. What I really needed was some positive attention and probably a good ole' butt whooping. So the first time I saw this dude on the block, he started calling me TJ Sparkle. I had no clue what that meant but it sounded good to me. I started to see him more frequently but never approached him because I didn't think it was appropriate. But, I did make sure I made myself noticeable. Friendly flirting. Plus, I heard he was into older women and would never be interested in lil' ole' me. He wasn't looking for a church girl. He wanted someone who was established. I

 was established in my studies and young foolishness.

Junior year, I am taking school a little more seriously. I always did well but I was moving into greatness. I knew I wanted to prepare for college and major in journalism. I created a plan. I did not have hands-on assistance at home or anyone in my neighborhood who knew how to navigate the process of higher education.

We had taken a break from selling candy out of my locker because of speculations of other illegal activities. We were starting to mature as young women trying to figure out what it was we wanted out of life. I was still boy crazy though; just more calm. We were preparing for ACT and SATs. I did great! I can't tell you my exact score but the colleges started calling. I was ecstatic because I knew the shift was about to occur. Yeah! A shift occurred but not the shift I imagined.

The bus rides home were the best. No one was beefing too much anymore. But, there was an incident where some of the older guys from the neighborhood were on the bus at the first stop. Now, I wanted to nudge the bus driver to figure out how he let these grown a$$ men on the damn bus without question. These men got full beards and war wounds. These men looked like they raised a tribe. You got to be kidding me. When we get to the second bus stop, the BDs get on and they get it cracking. Thornwood had just installed cameras on the bus because we were known for turning up really quick. It goes down in the DM, I mean on the bus. There is blood everywhere. One of the guys gets hit in the mouth with a 2x4. Another guy is hanging off the back of the bus with the emergency door opened.

It was a massacre. The driver was instructed to keep driving to the school where we will be met by local police. When things settled down I get called to the dean's office for questioning. I am tired of these run-ins. The dean asks me what happened. I am silent. I have nothing and I mean nothing to say. He turns on the video recorded on the bus' camera. All you see is me jumping from one seat to the next. I start laughing which caused me a Saturday detention. Bet you I had nothing to say though. You see the video just like I do so why do you need me?

Does anyone remember Washington Square Mall in Homewood, Illinois? That was my spot. That is where I got my first towel coat, Karl Kani outfit, and the Looney Tunes hoodie. The Diana was the movie theater and they had the arcade room. Venture's Department Store was right across the street. Those were the days. Remember Jubilation? I went once but after walking so far, it was time for me to go in the house. Ugh!

We had some fun rides home. Boys play fighting with the girls. Free feels all day. It was this short dude in particular who always made me laugh. Problem was, I could like him all day long but he was too short for me. We both had an interest in one another but I had something else going on after school.

You know that guy that nicknamed me TJ Sparkle? He became my boyfriend and on to be my baby daddy.

Some men are comfortable with you opening your legs but are uncomfortable with you opening your mouth – that ends NOW! ~ SJ   Tweet that! I mean really. Women aren't supposed to have a voice?

I was 16. He was 20. I thought I was grown. My n%^&* got a car, rims, sounds, and money. What y'all got? The situation was so messed up that we could not even see the problem. I was still a child in high school and he was grown. We even joked about how 16320, my mama's address, symbolized our ages and us having three children. I guess we should've changed my mama's address to 16220 because two children were born from this relationship.

He was dating an older woman while entertaining the idea of seeing me before we made it official. This woman came up to the school and parked outside my bus stop threatening me and telling me to stay in a kid's place. By this time, I was so full of myself and my mouth was raunchy. I could curse like a sailor. I could cut you without touching you. I was an official roaster. I am going to kill you with words before you have the opportunity to touch my soul. I was a soul-seeker.

Needless to say, she moved around. I felt like my childhood and teen years were invalid. During the day I was a high school student who flirted with boys I went to high school with; which was normal. But when I got off the school bus, my 20-year-old boyfriend is waiting for me with gifts. There was this one time where he had bought me a new coat after making fun of the childish coat my mama had bought me. I told him that instead of making fun he should buy me one. He did just that. When we were getting off the bus, he and his boys were face-down on the ground because the Jump Out Boys (plain clothed police officers) thought they were on garbage. They weren't.

Some of the girls on the bus like, "Dang, Qua-Qua your guy got you a coat and he stretched out on the ground!" Ha! Our relationship took off quickly. Almost too quickly for me. I was so torn. The friendly playful fights on the bus created feelings for some. For me, I had strong feelings for my school boo; the short guy on the bus.

So you know when you and your boo attend the same school, you have to share lockers. Now, this is the locker deal. Because my locker was close to all of our classes, we used my locker for everything. Like I said, it was our one stop shop. Me and one of my BFFs (I had two at the time, the other two main Roaches), wrote in this notebook about everything. She would take it to first period and write. I would take it to second period and respond.

But Mr. "I don't ever have any school supplies" decided to take the notebook to Mr. Butler's African American History class in order to take notes. I am referring to my school boo; the short guy on the bus. Now what you don't know is that what me and my BFF discussed in our secret notebook was our sexual encounters with our boyfriends, places we had gone, clothes we want, people we do and don't like, etc. We probably could have written a Zane book. I mean we talked about everything. And let me be the first to say, I was very imaginative when it came to sex. That's my truth. I promise you I could talk that talk and had even started walking it too (if you understand where I am going with this). I was sexually active with my 20-year old boyfriend. This wasn't a "we had sex one time – hit it and quit it" ordeal. This was a full blown every day after school until it was time for me to go home sexual relationships.

My BFF and I are panicking because when we return to the locker after class, we realized the secret notebook was gone. We leave to go retrace our steps and when we reconvene, the secret notebook is there. I get the notebook and take it with me thinking nothing of it. I'm just going to write and wait on a response. I open the book and there is another's person handwriting in the book. WTH! I mean this person has added comments on each page. This means someone knows everything! I'm in class rubbing my head. My hands are sweating profusely. It's time to go home for the day. I give the notebook to my BFF since I am going to enter my adult world as soon as I get off the bus. As I am giving her the book, I inform her that someone knows everything and was bold enough to comment.

Guess who comes and sits next to us on the bus and starts rubbing my leg? You guessed it. My school boo. He lets us know it was him so we can stop panicking. So we're sitting on the back of the bus staring at one another like damn. He now knows that I fantasize about him even in this relationship I'm in. I should have written a high school novel like my author friend, Jeffery Roshell (innocent plug) said. Go check him out! Side note: the secret notebook was so raunchy that the three of us had a private ceremony and burned the book a couple of years after graduating high school.

The stare he is giving me is so intense that we lock lips on the bus while BFF is on the lookout. To be perfectly honest, none of the relationships I have had with men were ever rooted in love. It was all lust. I had a lust demon so strong that derived from when I was 12-years old watching pornography that fed that lustful demon for 20 years. I came to terms to write this memoir when God freed me from this lustful demon. I am a 16-year old girl lusting for two different men.

This might not mean too much right now but I was only sexually active with my boyfriend. After the kiss with my school boo, we kept it cordial. We all kept writing in the notebook. It was therapeutic. It was a stress reliever and a distraction. As my junior year of high school came to an end, we all agreed that my BFF would hold on to the notebook.

While many found jobs that summer, I was busy being fast. All I cared about was living that 'hood life. I became very distant from my mother and no longer went to church and replaced it with running the streets with my boyfriend. I participated in his activities that were not always on the right side of the fence. I attended all of his family functions. When I was in the neighborhood, it was strange because I had drastically changed. His crowd had become my crowd. I went to all the car shows. I hung out at the car wash or shop where he hung out.

I did take drivers education that summer since I missed it my sophomore year. Poor driving instructor. I cannot remember his name but he passed me when he should've failed me ten times over. I pressed my foot on the gas when I should've pressed the brakes. I drove over an entire row of yellow parking bumpers while he was drinking hot coffee. Baby bye! I cried like a baby. I was so apologetic. I did not have good driving experiences during the practicing phase. I did not get my license until I was 19.

I had run into my school boo and it was disheartening to know that what I thought was lust turned into true concern for a friend. It was a typical crush a teenage girl had for a boy. I know our language was too explicit and inappropriate but we really cared for one another. Oh well!

We had one of those friendships that no matter who or what we were dealing with, we always had one another's back. We did not have to see each other on a daily basis to know the love and concern was there. The summer of '97 went by kind of fast.

Drum roll, please. It's my senior year of high school and yes, Shaniqua thinks she is grown. I met a real cool friend prior to my senior year of high school. My mama nicknamed her Pretty Girl. She had transferred from another high school and the newbies always catch hell. She stood up for herself and ruffled a few feathers along the way. She became my ace. I became the God-mother to her first child. We went on to South Suburban College together and shared some crazy times.

I had met quite a few good people while I was in high school that I see on a regular basis, not referring to Facebook. I mean we have true friendships. We shared some great memories. I was not as involved with extra-curricular activities as I should have but my grades were on point. One activity I loved was being a part of the school newspaper club (journalism team) during part of my junior and senior year. The one thing I hated was swimming in this one instructor's class. She was different. I stayed on my menstrual cycle in her class. Lies! I just didn't want to get in the water. That water was filthy. I don't care if you used enough chlorine that it burned your nose. I just couldn't do it.

Let me not forget one of the most thought-provoking high school experiences. Reality was and still is – is that racism exists. As long as there is a way to divide (race, economic status, educational and family background) racism will live. I was either a freshman or sophomore in high school when the football team was in the lunch line and all joking around. One of the Black football players said something to the effect of using the word "nigga". One of White football players quickly replied in a jokingly matter using the word "nigga" too! All hell broke loose. Roscoe, one of the oldest security guards at the school was out breath trying to diffuse the situation. The whole school turned up to the max. There were people running everywhere. The tallest guy who may have been on the football team if my mind serves me right, were tossing people left and right. They had shattered the glass window in the lunch room. I thought it was Plexiglas. I didn't know you could shatter Plexiglas. In all the excitement, I was still scared because I did not know how severe this situation was going to be.

I ran until I thought I needed an inhaler and lost one of my gym shoes in the process. I believe I had on my gym uniform too! The school was on lock down and all local law enforcement were called to the school. Eventually, we had to ride a bus we may have not been familiar with due to the circumstances at hand. I ended up walking home from South Holland, Illinois at 171st and Park Avenue to Harvey. I was exhausted. I don't think I made it to school the next day.

Well, back to my senior year memories. I kept my hair done and when my hair wasn't done, I had enough hair to wear it all in one slick ponytail with my baby hair swooped. I spent the majority of my weekends at the hairdresser who was cold with it if she was high on weed (marijuana). I wore French rolls with a red and black basket weave. I was always called to the Dean's office to take my hair down or to leave school. I wore the gold heart initial rings on every finger. I loved the character, Winnie the Pooh. That's where my oldest girl got her nickname from. I wore the Winnie the Pooh jewelry too! I wore either grey or blue contacts and had the SWV nails. The nail technician never had to cut the nails. I could barely wipe my a$$.

In my eyes, life was great because I remembered when none of the boys saw me as a girl of interest. Now, I was hot! A hot commodity. The boys used to see me as the funniest girl alive but never as the one to go to the dance with or the one to be booed up with. Me and my boyfriend wore matching jerseys or would wear the same color scheme. Did any of you ever wear matching outfits? That was the corniest thing ever.

My senior year, I had to make up one of my sophomore year gym classes I missed when I broke my ankle. It was to the point where I would keep my gym uniform on. At least my gym shoes were always on point. To this day, gym shoes are my fetish. All my other peeps were getting out of school early because they were enrolled in work study. I managed to work my number so I could swap one of my gym classes in order to enroll into work study. I worked one day at McDonalds in Hazel Crest on 183rd near Kedzie Ave.

They did not give me one bit of training and threw me right in the drive-thru window. Plus, I did not know how to catch the bus to travel back and forth. I still don't know how to catch the bus! The one day I did work, my boyfriend took me. He picked me up playing my favorite song at the time, Put Your Hands Where My Eyes Can See by Busta Rhymes. That was my joint!

Everyone is getting excited about senior prom and graduation while I'm beefing with one of the underclassmen because she said she was with my boyfriend for V-day, when I knew that to be a lie. You want to know how I know she was lying? Valentine's Day 1998 was a day to remember. He splurged on me and we were inseparable for the most part. I damn near lived with him. Everything was cool until I had to tell my mama I was pregnant. February 14, 1998, close to midnight I told my mother I was pregnant.

I had been away for as long as I could. He was happy; almost too happy. My mother did not cry. She wept. It's one thing when you know your child is out there but it's another when that little girl you tried to protect had or will have living proof of her sins. Being a woman of faith who's heavily involved in church can cause you to experience public hurt while other's sin goes unnoticed or so you think. Mama, I'm sorry. We did not have a house phone so I walked to the corner store payphone to call him over. He came within seconds. My mama asked him a few questions about his take on the matter. His response caused my mama to go in to a rage. He said he was happy and couldn't wait until our baby came. He went on to say that he was glad to know I was carrying his child. I wished I could have crawled under a rock. That was straight overkill. He was doing the most.

I had missed my period. My BFF had her driver's license so we went to Super K-Mart in Homewood. I stole the pregnancy test because I was too ashamed to walk around with a pregnancy test let alone go through the check-out line. We get in the car and she drives me to a vacant parking lot on the backroad so I can pee on the stick. She puts the stick on the dashboard and we sit and wait. There are two lines in each window. The lines weren't faded. They were bold. I was stuck. She was stuck. She drives me to his house and I give him the pregnancy test. He's happy and starts thinking of names. I was thinking we were going to name her Dashanae (Daw-Sha-Nay).

Out of fear, I left home when in actuality my mother never put me out. Well, not then at least. I put myself out. Because I did not keep my McDonald's job, I was back to my two gym classes and in school all day. I kept my pregnancy a secret until an incident occurred in gym. We had to run a mile every day. Each lap, you would collect a popsicle stick. I had bought the same color popsicle sticks the gym department had.

I was cheating and hustling. I was selling sticks when my classmates were in need. This gym thing was taking a toll on me. The incident occurred when we were playing volleyball. I loved volleyball.

One of the guys in my class accidently hit me in the stomach with the volleyball. Before I could say anything my BFF yelled, "You hit her in her stomach and she's pregnant!" What? Once my boyfriend got word of what happened, he and his boys had a talk with the guy who hit me because he wasn't as apologetic as I thought he should have been.

Well, now the world knows and I had to be removed from all gym classes. The biggest problem was that I was removed from my homeroom of over three years. What you mean I have to go to a special homeroom for pregnant girls? Why? I was now a pregnant senior in Ms. Hamm's homeroom. I no longer ate during n my regular lunch period or with my friends. The pregnant girls ate together in their own special assigned lunch. I had a special hall pass that gave me the ability to leave class or allow extra time to get from one class to the next.

So, now I am a secret. Did we have an underground hallway? Probably. I was too through. I was putting on a front as if I wasn't hurt but I was crushed.

My mother wrote all my brothers a letter to invite them all to dinner on a Sunday evening. The purpose was to tell all my brothers that I was pregnant. The oldest brother walked out without saying a word. He left his family stranded for hours. We later learned that he went to get tore up (drunk) with one of his longtime friends. The middle brother was calm and wanted to make sure our mama was alright. My youngest brother said his favorite words. "Cool out!" He went outside to smoke about half a pack of cigarettes.

Everyone was hurt. Everyone was disappointed. The little girl they helped raise was preparing to be a teen mother. I was 17 years old and as naïve as I was when I was five. I tried to front like it was all good.

Honestly, I was hurting on the inside. All along the college recruiters are calling. I decided I did not want to go to prom because I couldn't wear the dress I wanted. The dress I wanted to wear was too revealing. I couldn't see myself rocking a crucial a$$ dress with a big belly and swollen ankles that reminded me of my incident in '96.

I passed an opportunity of a lifetime to go to Southern Illinois University (SIU) for Journalism fall 1998. I explained to the recruiter and the advisor I had been working with for months my senior year of high school that I was pregnant and could not attend. Even with the devastating news which really was only devastating to me, the advisor had a remedy to all of my issues...my excuses; but I wanted to run behind my then unborn child's father.

Prom came and gone. It's time to take graduation pictures. My mother and I have reconciled our differences as far as my unborn child is concerned yet there were some deep rooted reservations I had with her. The day before graduation, my BFF and I go to Evergreen Plaza to shop for our special day. I decided to get my left cartilage pierced. I didn't get my ears pierced until I was 16 years old away with my church in North Carolina for a convention. My mother almost lost her mind and went ham on the person who was supervising me. This was no different. My mother was helping me put my cap on so I could leave early for the graduation procession. She noticed I was in pain when I would shrug when she was trying to place my cap on my head. That's when she saw my new piercing.

She refused to attend my graduation. She eventually came but I think it was deeper than a piercing. Come on now Mama. Through all the trials in these last four years, I still managed to graduate on time. At first, my high school counselor, Ms. Ciambrone said I wouldn't graduate on time because of the one credit short in gym. My mama made a special trip to the school to make face-to-face contact letting them know that there was no way possible I was going to wait to graduate.

Guess who else attended my graduation? My daddy. His great niece; my cousin graduated a year early. That was awkward. No matter what the circumstances, I was glad to know he was there. The next time I would see him after this day (June 6, 1998) was after I gave birth to my first child.

She may have been upset with me as well as disappointed but she still looked out for me.

She even gave me a graduation party for all my family and friends to attend. We had a great time. I received so many gifts. They still showed love to let me know that no matter what the circumstances were, I was loved.

Fall '98 I had the best baby shower ever. There was no judgment. Only love. That was probably the last time I spent quality time with one of my aunts who was also my mama's BFF. She passed in 2000 while I was pregnant with my son.

October 9, 1998 is when my journey of motherhood began. Patricia Odia High was born at 8:42 pm in one of the first maternity suite models at Ingalls Memorial Hospital in a room of family from both sides.

Her father and I began to experience distance when she was about six months old. Not too long after, we were no longer together or should I say that we were not in a relationship because we still were having sex. I thought I would die. Damn! I should've gone to SIU.

Chapter Eight

15800 S. STATE STREET

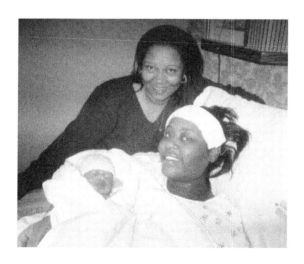

There were so many educational lessons and opportunities offered while attending South Suburban College off and on for ten years. Although I did not walk away with an associate's degree, I did earn over 75 semester credit hours and two certificates which paved the way for me to soar at Governors State University. I thought I was on the road to redemption after having my first child at 17 years old (6 weeks shy of

being 18 if that counts for anything). I had ended one dead relationship or so I thought with the father of my child. My mother and brother were great support systems from providing a roof over our heads to having a vehicle to drive to and from classes. I started a part-time job working at Wilsons' Leather in Orland Square Mall. The issues were that I had to rely on someone else to drop me off and or pick me up from work. To this day, I still owe this person an apology.

Attending South Suburban College was a constant reminder of high school and I felt as if I owed it to myself to relive my senior year since I was pregnant and missed those rewarding experiences. I barely attended classes my first semester. I spent more time in the cafeteria than I did in class. I was in the cafeteria running my mouth or participating in student life activities. I can hardly recall visiting an advisor to assist me in selecting classes until the end of my run at South Suburban College. This particular advisor is a woman I truly admire and have remained in contact to this present day. The thing for me was that I was able to maintain passing grades even in my absence. I was all right with being mediocre because I wanted to fit in with everyone else. I had become the bad chick who thought she was larger than life. My name was Qua-Qua and everyone knew it. I always said that I did not do drama but unfortunately, I did. I thrived on ignorance.

July 21st 1998
10:22 p.m

Qualita,

What's up dog? Hows the baby? Don't have the baby until I get home. Funny huh!! I don't really have much to say because I just talked to you about 4hours ago. Nothing much has changed since then..Be good!! 32,000 altitudio or whatever is boring as hell. I'm just sitting here listening to some slow jams, thinking: about life and what there is to come. Every since I don't know when we've wanted to hurry up and finish high school. Now that we're done what to do. I'm kinda' of scared to grow up and have real life problems. Just to be out in the world seems scary as hell. But what the hell growing up is a part of life. Well sorry the letter is so short but I really don't know what to write. And being the busy person that you are I don't want to occupy any more of your time. So take care until next time.

(Roach Love)   2 of um'!!!!

Love Always
Ladena

Sorry
loppy

My life was filled with drama and I accepted this as my reality. It seemed as if the more attempts I made to cross over to doing things the right way, the visits from my child's father became more frequent. Over the ten-year period at South Suburban College, my academics were a reflection of my personal life. I could never settle on a specific discipline. I originally strived to be a journalist then went on to business management/entrepreneurship. The list goes on to obtaining certifications as an administrative assistant and one other, courses taken in human services, computer, and the list goes on to cover multiple disciplines.

I learned the system quickly when it came to financial aid. I can admit that the disbursement checks were an added bonus to continuing my education but there was something missing. Drive! I did not have someone to explain the college process to me nor did I have someone to address the financial obligations to obtaining a degree. All I knew was that I was taking classes and socializing on a daily. After my first semester, I decided that I needed to rethink this whole school situation.

When I returned with a clear mind, I had not freed myself from a dysfunctional relationship with my child's father. We had one of those "we are not together, but we can still do us" type of relationships and that is what I settled for. I mentioned this early on where my mother kicked me out of her home. I promise I never thought that would happen, especially when I felt my daughter, her granddaughter was my "get out of jail" free card. I am thinking there is no way she would put me out on the streets with nowhere to go with her granddaughter. Rude awakening. I was sitting my narrow tail on her front porch blowing bubbles and kicking rocks expecting my mom to reconsider. Nope. Did not happen. I tried seeing other people to get over the hurt I experienced with my child's father but failed.

The only person available to take my daughter and me into their house was my child's father. I was straight pitiful. I had no will or motivation to be a responsible mother, daughter, sister, and employee, or student. I was a low life with no ambition. I had hoped for the successful conclusion where my child's father and I could look past our differences and make an amends. Not just to be cordial but to be a unit, a family. That did not last too long. I asked my mother if I could return home. I returned to South Suburban College, enrolled my baby into full-day daycare, and worked 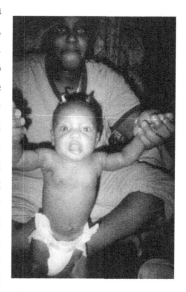 full-time at Speedway Gas Station in Homewood, Illinois as a cashier.

Life was beginning to look up for a sister until I started feeling nauseous in the morning. I thought the feeling came from working around all of the germs and chemicals. I began to lose my focus in class and could not sit through an entire lesson without gagging or excessively using the washroom. I soon found out what that feeling was….Patrick Odell High was born 10/26/2000. While I was pregnant with my second child, I experienced delayed post-partum depression, which I thought was a term I came up with on my own, but whatever.

I sought the expertise of a few adoption agencies because I felt there was no other way. I could barely care for one child with minimal assistance from my child's father and definitely took the shame notch up another level. Not to mention that the streets began to talk with accusations that my child's father might not be the father of my only born son. Now, hold up! This is not the Maury Povich Show; this is my life we are talking about.

Of course, I was out of school for a short period as I tried to make sense of what all had occurred. Still no degree. I lost the little stability and focus I had mustered up from my core. I had allowed this young man (children's father) to leave me hanging with not just one child but two…knowing damn well he had no intentions on repairing a broken relationship. Not necessarily with me as the mother of two of his children (you can tell the DNA results reflects that my son is his child) but to co-parent in a healthy manner.

Let me stop lying. I actually thought that he would make every attempt to meet me halfway and be the husband and father who thrived in making his family priority. That never happened and I fell into a deep depression.

What many never knew was that I suffered from bipolar depression (undiagnosed for some time before an actual diagnosis). From the age of 15, I had turned into another person. I struggled.

When I got back to South Suburban College, I took a different approach to take back everything I allowed the devil to steal from me. I started working at a family-owned restaurant in

Flossmoor, Illinois. I began to take my education seriously and I learned the steps of building a strong work ethic. I was able to apply theory learned in the classroom to practice as a manager of a restaurant. I earned this position as being a recipient of food stamps who qualified for a work program where they paid for my work uniforms and other benefits.

I thought I was in to something great. I thought I had found my balance. I believed I had regained the love and trust of my mother and brother. Unfortunately, I am just realizing at the age of 35 that what was lost cannot be restored to its original state but can be renewed with God's guidance. We have to learn to forgive ourselves and walk in the way in which God has set for us.

One of the hugest mistakes I made was when I knew some of the people in my children's father circle were interested in something I may have to offer (and it was not my mind), I entertained the lustful desires. One night, I decided to hang out with one of my best friends and two of the people from the circle. We rode around drinking and talking trash. We decided to go to a motel room and take the trash talking to the next level by putting our money (better yet, vajayjay) where our mouths were.

While my best friend and one of the people were in the bathroom, the other guy and I were in the bedroom. One thing led to another and the entire time I felt like a straight hoe knowing I only went this far to anger my children's father. I became overwhelmed with emotion during sex. My moans of lust turned into a plea for mercy. I wanted him to stop but he continued to delve deeper and deeper into my insides. I yelled, "NO!" yet he continued as if this is what I wanted and this is what I asked for. I can only imagine that he knew exactly the reason why I chose to hang with him at this particular time.

This still does not justify why he decided to keep digging into my guts. WTF!

Sidebar: I had no clue what it meant to "release" and I was in excruciating pain. The sheets were soaking wet and he explained in this turmoil that my body is reacting to him letting him know that no matter what words are coming out of my mouth that my body is telling him something different. I couldn't even tell you how long this fiasco took place but it felt like forever.

I don't give two flying horses what the situation is or why you chose to do what you do intimately with someone. When you are done and let the word flow from your mouth, "NO!" That's

just what it is. My best friend said she knew something didn't sound right and decided to open the bathroom door only to hear the difference between pleasure and pain. She ran to my rescue and the other guy told him how bogus he was for going too far. I had sunk so far down into the bed that I felt I was being pulled from a sea of forgetfulness. We all tried to make light of the situation as I ran to the bathroom with my friend while the guys argued about the circumstances at hand. The guy my friend was with exclaimed, "YOU RAPED HER!"

That is when I realized my NO was exactly that – RAPE! I had to come to terms that I was just raped. My best friend and I stayed in the bathroom cleaning my sins away but they were embedded into my skin through my pores. Sins cannot be cleaned by getting in the shower or taking a hoe bath. It just does not work like that.

When we walked out the bathroom, everything happened in slow motion. We stared at the bed and the wetness I felt was not a positive response to this dude entering my body but it was a pool of blood. There was so much blood that the blood had soaked through the mattress.

What part of the game was this? One life travesty after another created the devil's workshop in my mind. My best friend and I went to the emergency room and after waiting for several hours, I left. I thought that since we used protection and not losing too much blood (yeah, right) that I could survive by going home, crying into my pillow, and say the sinner's prayer would make everything alright. Of course, this was not the best idea, but when you are shamed and lack understanding and a self-esteem level not high enough to pull yourself together, you walk away from treatment.

After coming to terms with my truth as I put pen to paper, I see the trickle-down effect of issues leading to my suicide attempt.

I still managed to bounce back externally yet my soul was damaged. Only people that knew what occurred that unfortunate night was the four people in that bogus motel room.

Ha! You probably thought I was going to talk about higher education in this chapter given the title and address of South Suburban College. I cannot apologize.

Bounced back. Barely. I managed to carry on with the day-to-day hustle and reenrolled into school. This time, I became as involved as I can be in school. I buried my hurt and pain into my studies. I maintained a high grade point average of 3.0 or higher for several consecutive semesters. I worked as a student worker for career services and the counseling department. I found my flow.

One day this nice looking young man comes walking into the career services office looking for assistance with his resume. After helping him revamp his resume and providing additional job resources, he asked to keep in contact. I agreed. Here I am agreeing to some more nonsense.....I just did not know it yet. I thought I assessed the situation well.

Educated. Check.

Working. Check.

Well-groomed. Check.

Articulate. Check.

Fine as hell. Check.

Before you knew it, I was back to my promiscuous ways. Our  casual sex led to expectancies of more. During this period of time, I learned that my father was ill. I thought he was going to bounce back like he always did so I didn't make visiting him a priority. When I did visit him it was depressing to see the strong-willed man lying in a hospital bed withering away. Yet, I was in denial. I just knew he was going to live forever. The guy I was seeing was so supportive of me spending time with my father that it brought me even closer to him. That was a tactic he pulled out of his back pocket. I was too naïve to even see what was really going on.

I found out I was pregnant with my third child by this young guy I thought I knew because I had spent so much time with him. Two weeks after finding out I was pregnant with child number three, my father passed away on April 19, 2003. Child number three, Ayanna was born on January 7, 2004, after three days of hard labor. Through these abrupt changes, I continued to attend school even during this high-risk pregnancy. Those grades were still on point and I was even recognized as a student leader and scholar. While pregnant, I was afforded the opportunity to represent the college at a student leadership conference in Boston, Massachusetts.

When I delivered the news that I was pregnant with my third child, I just knew I was going to experience the heartache of knowing he was going to deny this child. To my surprise, he did the total opposite. He began to make plans based on us being a blended family; my two oldest children, our unborn child, and the two of us. What? Did you just hear the words coming out of my mouth, sir? Do I finally get the family I longed for but with a new person and a new child on the way?

The staff at South Suburban College were the best. I was allowed to perform light work in the financial aid office. Many of my academic needs were accommodated through the support of instructors and staff. No one judged me for they knew very

little of my troubled past and current situation. They could only see the determination and the drive to excel beyond my circumstances.

Sound good! We were married in Crown Point, Indiana on November 19, 2003 prior to my third, his first child's birth. My mother and brother were devastated with all of the events that transpired in that short period. He was everything I thought we needed in our lives. He could cook and he was very attentive to our needs. That was short lived because I learned some of his family dynamics that blew my mind.

I learned that he struggled with an addiction to drugs. Shortly after being married, life took a turn for the worse. When I mustered up the pride and courage to leave, I learned I was pregnant with child number four. With his drug addiction becoming more noticeable, we lost our apartment and all of our belongings. I can recall the many times we had to move from one location to another. My mother even allowed us to move in with her hoping we could get it together. Here I am again on bended knee asking for mercy because I cannot go on living this way.

 On the outside, everyone thought he was the ideal husband and father until his addiction took control. He had managed to steal from everyone I knew; causing havoc every corner we turned. People began to distance themselves to prevent any issues with us.

I tried to stick it out with him through his battle but I was only enabling him. I tried to keep his addiction a secret because I was not raised in or around this type of chaos. I thought I had an image to uphold. Qua-Qua with a crackhead? Nah! That don't even sound right.

The people who helped me the most through this turmoil were growing tired of my mess and my inability to let go. How in the hell was I going to raise four children all alone? I was blinded to the reality of the stress and anxiety I had endured. I began to age and gain excessive weight. One of the strongholds between us was the ill-thought of when I attempted to have a successful abortion when I learned I was pregnant with child number four. We were living at my mother's home trying to get on our feet. We shared this moment and allowed this one detrimental moment hold us to one another. I had made a conscious decision that I was going to have an abortion. He drove me to this bootleg abortion clinic and everything in me was telling me to leave. The women were going on and on about partying that same night after having an abortion. WTF! After completing a short intake form and ultrasound, the nurse explained to me that the procedure was NOT 100% guaranteed. I'm thinking, I never heard of anyone experiencing any issues

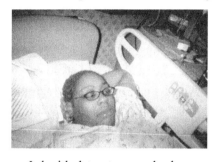

and once the procedure was done that was it....that's all. I signed the consent and waiver form agreeing to all of the terms (even the small print). The cost was more if you wanted to be put to sleep so I decided to stay awake because not only could I not afford to be put to sleep, I wanted to see everything they were doing.

My time came to have the abortion. He was able to accompany me to the back while I lay still on the table as they inserted a vacuum-like tube in my vagina. Can you imagine what it felt like to literally have your soul ripped from your vital organs? As I lay almost lifeless on the table, the tears flowed so heavy filling the openings of my ears. I was drowning in sorrow, pity, and disappointment.

Once the procedures was over, I received instructions on aftercare, follow-up appointment, and a prescription for an antibiotic. There was complete silence on the way home. No fighting. No desire to initiate an argument. Just peace in the midst of the storm. I returned to work the next day as if nothing ever happened the day before. A few of my coworkers knew what had happened and gave me comfort in knowing that whatever decision I made was just that; my decision. The next week, I went to my follow-up appointment. He came with me. The nurse performed an ultrasound and gave me the normal patient/provider spill. But there was something peculiar about her tone and posture that had changed within the matter of moments. She asked to be excused and said that she would return in a few minutes. When she returned, she had another nurse with her who seemed to be a little more seasoned than she was. They both mumbled some words and abruptly walked out. My ex-husband began to get antsy and walked out to find someone who can tell us what was going on.

My ex-husband, the two nurses, and a doctor walked in to inform us that I was pregnant with twins; one child behind the other reflecting a sound of one heart beat only. While I terminated one pregnancy, the other child remained. Yeah, just like that! In that moment, I was reminded of being a child raised in church where the elders told me that there was something unique about me. There will be things that others can get away with (or so I thought) that I would not have the luxury of doing. When you are called, you can do all you can to run from the calling, but He will get your attention one way or another. Many called. Few chosen.

I felt like the smallest person in the world. I could not even fathom the news that I just received. My ex-husband is balling with tears and anger yet giving me the vibe that he should not have supported this foolery in the first place. Needless to say, child number four was born February 5, 2005. During this pregnancy, I learned I had cervical cancer via Human Papillomavirus (HPV). One too many abnormal pap smears is a sign that you need additional care. Do NOT neglect your body or become numb to medical news that is displeasing only to avoid receiving the necessary medicinal attention.

Here I am, age of 24 with four children, married to a drug addict, facing cancer head on, working full-time as a bank teller, missing higher education, which was my safe place….broken and lost.

The day I went into labor with child number four, my ex-husband stole all of my jewelry that I had to remove per the doctor's orders. He ran off with my brand new van my mother purchased on my behalf because I missed the income requirements  by $60. I paid the car note but once again, I had to depend on my mama and she came to my rescue. I was driving this beat up car that I had to use a screwdriver to start the car. I believe I could only make right turns after driving it for several months. I was pitiful.

So, he runs of with my van to get high. When he finally returns, the van is on a donut and my jewelry had been pawned. Whyyyyyyyyyyyyy???

What I haven't mentioned is that he was abusive towards me. After so long and excessive weight gain, I began to fight back to the point where I enjoyed fighting him. I would beat the breaks off of him and thrived off every minute of it. It would get so bad that the police would be called and I would be taken to the police station. This had become my way of life. Every weekend, someone was coming to bond me out if I did not get an I-bond. My babies would be with my mother or a friend.

He rarely went to the police station because the evidence of his cuts, bruises, and broken bones forced many officers to take me in opposed to him being removed. Plus, in my younger years I had plenty of run-ins with the local police officers. They had it out for your girl. Hell, I had it out for myself!

I had to learn to forgive myself in order to forgive him. Our marriage was short lived, but it felt like an eternity. There were so many turning points while in this wilderness that it was by God's grace and mercy that I made it thus far. I couldn't have made it without Him. Mama, thank you for praying for me.

You get the gist of my living hell.

I continued a few semesters at South Suburban College before completely transitioning to old stomping grounds. I kept my promise from when I was in middle school. I promised to return to Governors State University. I didn't think I was going to ever make it back there after experiencing all of these obstacles, but I made it with God on my side.

When I tell you, writing my life on paper and piecing together the fragments of my broken heart allows me to fully experience The Potter. The Potter wants to put you back together again.

In case you have fallen by the wayside of life
Dreams and visions shattered, you're all broken inside.
You don't have to stay in the shape that you're in
The potter wants to put you back together again,
Oh, the potter wants to put you back together again.

In case your situation has turned upside down,
And all that you've accomplished, is now on the ground.
You don't have to stay in the shape that you're in
The potter wants to put you back together again,
Oh, the potter wants to put you back together again.

You who are broken, stop by the potter's house.

You who need mending, stop by the potter's house
Give Him the fragments of your broken life,
My friend, the potter wants to put you back together again,
Oh, the potter wants to put you back together again
Joy in the potter's house.
Peace in the potter's house.
Love in the potter's house.
There is salvation in the potter's house.
There is healing in the potter's house.
There is deliverance in the potter's house.
You'll find everything you need in the potter's house.
The potter wants to put you back together again,
Oh, the potter wants to put you back together again.

Walter and Tremaine Hawkins
Songwriters:
VARN MICHAEL MCKAY
© Universal Music Publishing Group
For non-commercial use only.

We cannot change the past, but we can change our attitude toward it. Uproot guilt and plant forgiveness. Tear out arrogance and seed humility. Exchange love for hate — thereby, making the present comfortable and the future promising. ~ Maya Angelou

Eliminating Racism. Empowering Women. YWCA: http://www.ywca.org/site/c.cuIRJ7NTKrLaG/b.9360173/k.108 9/YWCAEliminating_Racism_Empowering_Women.htm

Chapter Nine

6634 S. DREXEL

Through the Years
(Tuesday, October 10th, 2006)

I know we have been through a whole lot through the little time we have spent together. I pray that no matter what ups and downs I may experience and take you through, we will always remain close. There has been times when you wanted to question different decisions I chose to make but, you trusted my judgment whether I am right or wrong. I will always be your mother and you will always be my children (**Patricia, Patrick, Ayanna, Ariel,** and Sanaa). When you all get older there are plenty of things I would like to tell you and teach you for your own good.

I dedicate this letter to you now for the future and always, even when I am gone. This is not a sob letter, this is a letter to let you know that each one of you hold a special place in my heart. I have had my share of changes and obstacles. When I thought of doing foolishly my mind reflects like a mirror and I see all of you. I thank God for giving all of you to me. There is no telling where I would be if God did not give you to me as your mother.

Patricia you were the first born child (that gave me a wake up call and a challenge). You were born @ 8:42 p.m. on October 9th, 1998. I was 17 years old (6 weeks shy of being 18). We would walk outside early in the day into the night just to keep you happy. Oh! Don't forget to mention how Be-Be (Grandma Lovingood) came over everyday to see her **Pooh**. You were flourished with the nicest things a little girl could hope for. You were also the first born grandchild in the house (16320 S. Carse, Harvey, IL. 60426). You were the one who started the name Ga-Ga. She always will be Ga-Ga (Grandma Anderson, my mom). Patricia, you are a people person, hilarious and a go - getter. I love you, **Pooh**!

Patrick you are my second born child. You were the quietest baby that I have had until you learned how to walk. You were born @ 4:10 a.m. on October 26th, 2000 (a millennium baby). My only son, too. Your hospital pictures prompted us to nick - name you **Chef**. The picture will explain the name. I named you **Patrick** thinking you and **Patricia** were going to be the only two children I gave birth to. Ha! Ha! Ha! Guess not. As you get older you seem to be more and more like your Uncle Rod...who was like a father to me. You are so wise and little do you know, I take your word for a lot of things that you don't even realize.

You are a wise, intelligent, and a unique individual. You always said that you were going to be a preacher and a big brother to all of your sisters, I believe you. I love you, **Patrick!**

    Ayanna my dear , I was in labor with you for 3 long and painful days. I would not trade you for the world. Mama (Ga-Ga) calls you Jefferson since you look so much like her side of the family. You were born @ 9:11 a.m. on January 7th, 2004. You are like the only child that looks similar to me, you also look like Patrick too. (You started the name bru- bru for Patrick). We call you **Ya-Ya** for short and don't let no one forget it. **Yanna** you are very athletic to be so young and set in your ways **Ms. Boss**. You give **Patricia** and **Patrick** a run for there money. On your father side of the family you are the first born grandchild. People always compliment on how smart you are and how you pronounce your words so well. I love you, **Ya-Ya!**

    Ariel, what can I say? You came at a very crucial time in my life and having you turned out to be one of the best blessings I can ever receive. We have a lot to talk about when you get older, **Arie**. You were born @ 3:37p.m. on February 5th, 2005. You look so much like your father, I should've named you Carlita (not!). We moved around so much when you were born, I thought we were part of a circus (not really). To be honest you are the feistiest of them yet. Right now at this present time, you have grown past your sister, **Ayanna**. Your big sister, **Patricia** and you are the cat'ent ups of the group. Sorry for rushing your baby times because, mommy has another baby on the way. You are still special sweetheart. I love you, **Arie!**

    Last but not least, Sanaa. You are not here yet but, we have a lot to talk about as well. When you get here you will finally get the chance to meet the woman who has carried you for 8 or 9 months. You must be a blessing to pass the shot (birth control). The ultrasound says you are supposed to be a girl. If right, I am naming you Sanaa, which means beautiful; work of art. I love you, Sanaa!

    Five beautiful children that I would not trade even on my worst day. Mommy, has a few issues she needs to work out with God leading me. I wish you all the best in life and I am here to help you accomplish all of your dreams and aspirations. Hold your head up high, for you all are Chosen. Chosen to live right and to walk by faith and not by sight. God is everything and without him we are nothing, remember this always. He comes first and the rest will follow. A family that prays together will stay together, too. Love you all, Mommy (Shaniqua).

One thing I did not mention in chapter 6 was a fight that occurred in the latter part of 2004 while I was pregnant with child number four. Although this has nothing to do with 6634 S. Drexel, I felt I may have left you hanging. This incident occurred at my mom's home: 16320 S. Carse. The fight was between me, my middle brother (the one we call father), and my ex-husband. To this day, I still cannot tell you if this was a set-up or what because it didn't even seem real. My youngest brother had invited my family over because we had extended family coming over from out-of-town. I think we probably had gotten there too late but we made it nonetheless.

When we get inside, my three brothers are in the basement talking and drinking (alcohol). My youngest brother, the jokester, makes a comment about us showing up late and we all laughed. Then he goes on to ask me about my due date, etc. Small talk. Cool. My middle brother decides to chime in and goes off on a tangent calling me a WHORE, BABY MACHINE, BROKE BITCH, DUMB FUCK......the list goes on to him using words I had no clue was in his vocabulary. Straight low blows. The two other brothers are trying to calm him down while my ex-husband is getting amped up. My youngest brother's wife asks me and my family to leave and we do just that.

I'm balling, crying uncontrollably while my ex-husband drives us to my mom's home about 10-15 minutes away. We get to my mom's and I tell her everything that happened, word-for-word. As we are processing what happened because this is so out of character for the middle brother, he enters the front door. He's hollering and scaring my babies. He repeats the same harsh words as if I needed a do-over. Ha! This time, there is no other brothers to stop him or my ex-husband just yet. My middle brother walks up to me and I guard my stomach because I do not know his next move. My ex-husband jumps up to stay as close to me as possible. In that moment, wait; let's take a long pause.....my brother coughs up phlegm from his soul and spits it on my right cheek. The spit...phlegm or whatever you want to call it was so thick that I could not easily wipe it off. That's when my ex-husband threw the first punch. My mother tried to step in between them but was tossed to the side. This is going all wrong. My intentions were to run to Mama as always and be the first to make my point hoping to be believed. It was one of those "if I tell my side of the story first, you will believe me" type of ordeals. Moments later, my other brothers show up. We are asked to leave my mom's home and we do just that, again! We get outside and I am trying to get

 the three babies situated in the car. Meanwhile, my middle brother charges out the front door and runs up on me. The ex-husband knocks him out and stomps his head into the ground. In rage, I help until I do not see my brother moving anymore. We were all out of control. My mother told me to never come back to her home and to lose her number.

By this time, some of you may agree that I had one too many children. My middle brother was right about some of the things he said but his delivery was way off. Did I ever believe in birth control? Yes. I was on birth control when I found out I was pregnant with child number four. I was on the birth control shot when I found out I was pregnant with child number five. Huh!

Being a responsible individual means holding yourself accountable. What are you held accountable for? This form of narrative writing has brought me to terms with my reality. Thank God for never giving up on me.

Be careful how much of you –you compromise to fit in. Set yourself FREE!

Fast Forward. One thing I learned in this position is that when you ask for promotion, you are asking for problems. Can you handle it?

Well, let me get to it. Address 6634 is where I spent close to 6 years in the nonprofit sector working with formerly incarcerated men who battled addiction. These men and my former boss taught me to humble myself and become more compassionate for others who struggle with issues that differ from my own. And, we all have sinned and caused harm…mine just differs from yours.

There is a difference between if you've ever committed a crime and if you've ever been convicted of one. Crime = sin

We all have sinned. Based on how the question is answered will determine how we respond.

Is there a difference in your response?

In 2006, I was pregnant with my fifth child; the last of the Mohicans. I was making one final attempt to save my ex-husband. Key word; save. Who am I? I can't save anyone. Jesus saves. That was my biggest problem. I had a misconception of what marriage was supposed to be. I had a fear of being alone raising four soon-to-be five children. One failed attempt after another resulted in taking a different approach.

This different approach worked in my favor in the long run but I can't speak on his behalf regarding the outcome. God bless him!

One summer day in 2006, I accompanied my ex-husband to a male recovery home located on the south side of Chicago. We took a tour of the facility and after an agreement with him receiving the needed help, we completed the intake process.

The intake process was lengthy and somewhat intimidating if you are not familiar with the language and processes. I made a few detailed suggestions that sparked the interest of the executive assistant.

The next day, I received a call from the recovery home. I'm thinking it has something to do with my ex-husband relapsing (I had no hope...honestly). I was just going with the flow. The call came from the executive assistant who was impressed with my demeanor and professionalism. Who me? Are you referring to this ghetto chick from Harvey with all these kids? She had spoken highly of me to the executive director who wasn't fond of the idea of me working at the recovery home part-time due to my ex-husband being a client. I understood the conflict of interest.

 The executive director decided to take a chance on me. I am glad I was able to use the knowledge learned at South Suburban College to articulate what was missing from the intake process and being more inclusive to approach when working with this special population. These men were considered the forgotten.

I started working part-time on July 18, 2006. My mother almost lost her life July 19, 2006. She had a hernia over 60 plus pounds erupt and almost choked her to death. I found my mother lying on the living room floor of her home dying. I immediately called 9-1-1 for help. She was rushed to the hospital and the doctors made a decision to repair the hernia than to remove because of the risk and complications involved.

I thought I had lost my mama forever. God is not through with her yet.

I managed to go to work the next day because I did not want to dwell in sorrow nor did I want to miss this opportunity to work this new gig. Plus, how realistic would that have sounded if I called in with a "my mama's in the hospital, can't come in" phone call? I know I would have been able to provide documentation of the truth, but this lady (executive assistant) took a chance on me and I do not want to disappoint.

My mother was admitted into the Intensive Care Unit (ICU) and later transferred to a regular room for recovery after a few weeks. I thought she was returning home, but this surgery was more serious than my family was willing to admit. My mom remember this day because when she was released to be transferred my children are happy and are chanting, "That's my Gaga. We love Gaga." I was happy for them and for myself. Now we are on the road to recovery.

Mom was admitted into a rehabilitation center for several more weeks. While my mother was recovering, I was dying. I was grasping for air. I saw my mother as my Earthly protector who could cover me during my trials. I felt like she was my oxygen tank. I relied too heavily on my mom. I was pitiful!

She was doing great in rehab. Here, I have a spouse in recovery and my mom in rehab. I am six-months pregnant with four children ranging from the ages 1-7 trying to work part-time and care for everyone but myself. My brothers could only hold on to the fond memories from when our mom was a young whipper snapper. I have learned that my immediate family loves holding on to the past. For real, for real.

In the meantime, my mother is discharged from rehabilitation. I am so happy! I am overjoyed! The only issue was that I would have to care for her without any assistance. She had an open wound where two bulbs hung from each side of her stomach to drain the infection. As her recovery weighs heavily on my mind, I had to be mentally and emotionally present at work.

Currently at the gig, I am working on an upcoming state audit where I had to manage client files to ensure they were organized in a particular order. For some client files, I had to reach out to them and other agencies to complete the follow-up process. We passed the audit with flying colors with high recommendations to continue receiving grant funds.

While the position was only to be temporary, I was asked if I wanted to stay on board part-time in hopes of becoming full-time if I decided to come back the next year after giving birth to my baby girl. I kindly accepted because I had begun to make some changes to the procedures in place as well as updating the intake forms. I started building a rapport with Illinois Department of Corrections, Chicago Department of Public Health, Illinois Department of Human Services (Department of Alcohol and Substance Abuse (DASA)), and other state and federal agencies. With a successful audit came a nice promotion. I was loving this.

I worked days and cared for my children and mother in the evening. Big props to my two oldest children for helping their mommy! My son was and still is a tremendous help and he doesn't get enough credit for all he has done. So I'm doing me and preparing to have my baby in the next few months. Yes, I was overwhelmed but staying busy kept me going. An idle mind is the devil's workshop.

I am starting to conduct phone interviews with men who are being released from IDOC or those seeking housing or who are struggling with addiction. A client who was misplaced due to not meeting the criteria of our housing program was offered a job as a house manager not too long after arriving. This guy was different than any other encounter I ever had with a man. I know I sound like my promiscuous side but guess what? I DO NOT care! Transparency is also a part of my intimate journey. I have to be transparent. You've paid your money for this great read and I am not going to short change you. This is my truth! Don't get me wrong, I was hesitant when writing this particular chapter but I know God got me.

This young man would genuinely ask me how I was doing and more importantly what I was doing with my life. He would inquire about my due date, if I was having twins (because I was enormous), if I needed anything, etc. I guess you could say he was my work husband. They do exist. He stayed to himself and operated in a manner of integrity. Enough about him.

Not too long after my mother was released home, my ex-husband has relapsed and could no longer reside in the recovery home. He moves back "home." Back to hell again. My mother allowed my ex-husband to live with us because I had become my mom's caretaker. How foolish was I to allow this drama back in my mother's home while she make an attempt to recuperate from a life-altering procedure? I will say this; my ex-husband was very helpful during this time. So much so that one afternoon when I went into my mother's  room to clean her, something smelled like a dirty diaper. I may not have been the cleanest person but one thing I did not do was leave dirty diapers lying around the house. I went to pull my mother up from her bed and when I counted to the number three, her incision opened wide and the infection poured out like an erupting volcano.

Ex-husband was like Johnny on the spot. It was so toxic and reeked death that when the Emergency Medical Technicians (EMTs) arrived, they paused before entering the house to mentally prepare themselves for war. Side note: my ex-husband caused me and my family a lot of grief but he was quick and had no reservation in cleaning the mess no one wanted to touch. I was too outdone! I could not even fathom what all had occurred. So, back to the drawing board!

Guess who still went to work until it was time to have her baby? Me! God kept my mother through it all. Mind you, my mother is the type to pray things through opposed to seeking medical attention. So for her to successfully make it through this part of her journey, I am still proud of her even though she sathinks I am not. The disheartening part of it all is that I tried to hold on to a failing marriage. I asked God while I was in labor with my baby girl that if He allowed

me to make it through this child birth I promised to gracefully walk away from this toxicity. On November 22, 2006, my 26th birthday, I gave birth to my baby girl, Sanaa Grace. I was in so much mental turmoil that I had to have an emergency Caesarean-section (C-section). The blessing was that I was able to have a tubal ligation as well. I consider this a 2-for-1. Thank you God!

Now, I needed a game plan to terminate this marriage. I made every attempt to be nice and cordial as well as informing him that this can no longer be. He started tripping out on me. I should've taken a different approach. But what would have that looked like? I am trying to bounce back and prepare to go back to work. I have all the paperwork complete for the children to attend daycare before and after school. All shot records are up to date.

Here this dude is all in his feeling scaring the living s$%^ out of me and my babies. He started appearing everywhere we were. For a dude with no wheel, he sure knew how to navigate the city. He knew everything about my mother's house, my kicking-it spots, work, daycare, where I did laundry.... EVERYTHING! He would stand at my bedroom window listening to my phone conversations. He would jump out of the bushes on me. It had got so bad that when I returned to work, he started showing up and creating a circus show. He would call the office phone and yell obscenities, "FAT BITCH, WHORE, TRICK!" I was too outdone. I would call the police to file a report, but because the business line is a public line, I could not file any stalker or harassment charges. My boss told me that this was too much at his place of business but had a remedy. They exchanged words too! My boss requested the young man I spoke of in the beginning of this chapter to work the same hours I worked to protect me.

The young man who protected me told me the raw truth. He told me that I had too much potential to be wasting my life dealing with peasants. He told me that I needed to nurture my children and become my own woman, not the woman someone else thinks is ideal. He told me I had a distinctive smell as if I did not properly wash clothes. He told me the wigs I was wearing was a mechanism to hide and that the s%^& was played out. He told me that I needed to smile more even though I had a small stain on one of my teeth. He told me that I needed to go up half a size in my shoes. He told me that I needed to take the time to pamper myself even if he had to sit in the car with my babies. Who does that? And just because you were sent to protect me does not give you the right to tell me about myself. Let me quit playing. I was fascinated by his words ever since that moment. He even told me that I did not know how to cook. How's that? My brothers ate my cooking. I guess that didn't carry no weight. Ha! Ha!

I'm still living at my mother's home and we have had to make some changes as she heals. Her bedroom was temporarily moved to the living room while my brothers fixed some small damages. Plus, this gave people the opportunity to visit in a more open space. The living room was equipped to meet her mobility needs. She was ready to manage her personal business with little to no assistance. Proud of my boo! But the devil was lurking and things were going too good.

I am making pretty good money working full-time and had just received another raise. I'm killing the game (with no benefits). To treat myself and the babies, I decided to buy portable TVs for my van. This way, I can listen to my tunes in peace while they watch their favorite movies. I'm thinking that was cool to do since I could remove them every day without the thought of them being stolen by the one and only ex-husband of mine.

I'm trying to be slick by hiding the TVs under the kitchen countertop with the pots and pans to make sure Mr. Clever don't get any ideas. But you can't out slick a slickster. The babies and I get home from a long day and I go to check to make sure the TVs are where I hid them. Nope. They are gone. Immediately, I grabbed the thickest belt I could find and called him into our room like he was a child. I work too hard. I go through too much and hustle my a$$ off to have something for me and my babies to enjoy. I whipped that brother like he was my personal slave. I whipped him like he was going to be stoned afterwards.

I'm not glorifying what I did but at that point, I had lost it. My oldest brother had to come in our bedroom and pry me off of him. Have you ever gotten one of those whippings where your mama, daddy, grandma, whoever would talk with a rhythm as the belt hit your body? Don't – you – ever – in – your – life – do – that – again! We all put him out. Brotha, you gots to go. You are not welcomed here.

We could never find him but knew he was lurking nearby. I am leaving work one day and realize my tire is wobbling but I am trying to get to my babies at daycare. I worked on the south side of Chicago and I need to make it to 167th & Woods by

6pm in order to prevent paying a late charge of $1 per minute per child. Right! I am amped up, listening to my music, and singing (so I think) aloud. I get to about 111th on the Dan Ryan and lose control of my van. I am swerving in and out of traffic. All I can do is hold the wheel and plead the blood of Jesus like my mama taught me. My van is going up the hill into the grass back down towards traffic and the concrete embankment. This goes on for a few minutes. My van finally stops right before the 119th exit less than an inch from the concrete embankment.

My initial thought was, Am I alive? I am thinking furthers let me know, Yes, I am alive. Plus, I can feel the sweat dripping from my hands down my arms to my elbows. Did you know my hands sweat profusely whether I am nervous or not? I have no control over this matter. The state trooper is yelling, "Miss, are you alright? Let's call someone in your family? Do you know who and where you are? You are going to need a tow truck!" The van is towed and my oldest brother comes to my rescue. All of my brothers are different and each one came to my rescue in their own ways. My oldest brother stuck it out with me when I was dealing with the craziness of my ex-husband. My middle brother is the rationalizer and assisted financially for needs. My youngest brother is the jokester who makes light of every situation. His favorite line is, "Cool out!" The tow truck company informs us that someone deliberately loosened all the lug nuts on all four tires. I wonder who. So, we playing the death game. I'm cool on all that. I never took any of this seriously because had I; I would've been admitted into the Wyman & Gordon Building (facility for the mentally ill). I just prayed and kept it moving.

This way of life had become my norm and I settled with this way of living for so long. I dragged all my people into my mess too! Damn!

It had gotten so bad that the children knew he had to be close or was in the vicinity because he smelled like 211 (malt  liquor/beer) and must. I'm in my newly repaired van back rolling and taking my babies to daycare when we realized that he must have slept in the van the night before. Two of the youngest girls (his biological children) said, Mommy, Daddy was here in our van, wasn't he?" I replied, "Yup, I am pretty sure of that." So, back to our regularly scheduled program. I drive the babies to daycare and get them in safely. I get back in my car headed to work on the south side [south side, south side (like the song)] Okay! Never mind. I'm driving down to 159th & Woods when he appears right behind me and tries to choke me with his bare hands. Fam, you got me bent if you think I am going out like this. I'm laughing and choking to keep myself calm. We tussle and as he gets out the car and runs, a police officer realizes that I am in distress, catches him and takes him into custody.

While we were asleep one night, my ex-husband broke into the house and stole a few items. Shaniqua (yeah, I am speaking in third person) is blind as a bat. All I can see is his image as he runs out the back door. We call my middle brother and the police. We realized the money my mother had hidden for some time was gone. Her evangelist license was gone too. Playa, you had to take the license too? Wow! After that night, it was one issue after another.

Guess who went to work after almost losing her life? Me! You guessed it. You know what? I was just as crazy if not crazier than he was. I thought our routine was, you try to kill me, I survive, and I go to work. That's it. That's all. He showed up at my job accusing me of sleeping with the clients. Boy, if you don't move all the way around. A sistah just got another raise and you pulling this type of garbage? Cool! I defuse the situation by telling him to get in the van and calm down. It wasn't because he stated truth but I don't need him messing up my money. Plus, I knew that look in his eyes. He was in distress. He looked suicidal. Now, as much turmoil he caused in my life, I couldn't help but see the hurting child he once was.

I knew his past. Some of which I wish I had never known but this man was troubled. We both were fighting demonic oppression. He had his battles. I had mine. I asked him where he wanted to be dropped off but he wanted to see the girls. Nah, partna'. Not in your condition. I was too afraid to get on the expressway with him in the van so I took the side streets. Too much!

He's asking me to take him back and to not go through with the divorce. He's throwing a tantrum in the van. Here we go! He starts yelling and telling me that he is going to jump out of the van while I am driving. Really? Me being the fool I was, I tell him, "Well, I might as well speed up!" He doesn't make it any better because he agrees. What does Shaniqua do? She speeds up. I am doing approximately 65 mph in a 30 mph zone. What does he do? He jumps out the van. Two fools lost with no cause. I have never seen smoke come from a person's body unless I was watching the road runner in the cartoons. His body is rolling down the street as I look in my rearview mirror. I cannot make this stuff up.

I pull over really quick to make sure I am straight and that no one thinks I have anything to do with what just happened. I call my big brother. He tells me to pull into a particular neighborhood and sit there until he gets to me. He comes directly to where I am and we switch vehicles. The game plan was for my brother to pick up the babies from daycare and to meet me at my mama's house.

Cool. Everything is going according to plan. With my brother having a military background, he's good for giving out order and demands. He was in ARMY mode. So my brother and I are explaining what happened to our mom. She's baffled and looking at us sideways hoping we didn't take this dude out. We didn't, just in case you are wondering.

The road-runner (ex-husband) comes knocking on the front door all bandaged up with holes in the knee of his pants and the sole lifted up off one of his shoes. Imagine this! This dude has to be immortal because how did you recover from your tumble just that fast. My brother told him to stay as far away as possible before someone seriously gets hurt.

I pulled myself together and started the process to file for divorce. I represented myself. I followed all the processes the clerk told me to. I posted my petition to file in the Chicago Law Bulletin. I submitted all one million documents, appearing in court, and following up with counsel as needed. Friday, May 16th, 2008, my divorce was finalized and I was a free agent...I mean woman. I am Shaniqua Anderson.

Now just because we were divorced did not mean his foolishness stopped. He would show up at the laundry mat until the young man I was talking about early on volunteered to wash all of our clothes which gave him a chance to teach me how to properly wash. As long as this young man was around, the coast was clear. This young man became my best friend, my partner. I'll be honest, I loved this young man but knew the lustful spirits in me would overtake the genuine love and concern I had for him. I had enough going on but he took the time to be a friend when I had no one. I had God all along but I was too silly to tap into my resource; God.

The closer this young man and I became, the further the ex-husband was. Except, the one scare where he tried to take the babies from school without my permission. Because I did not want to involve the school in my marital affairs, they had no clue of the extent of what was going on. Within the same hour, the babies were returned with no signs of harm. Do you remember Mr. Skubal, my grade school principal? Well, he was the one who resolved this particular issue and was very attentive to our needs once he knew what was going on.

I began investing in myself and my craft to help these men reintegrate back into society.

I learned how to do the billing and maintain the case notes for the clients. I started scheduling one-on-ones with the clients to address their individual needs. I was cold with linking the men with external agencies which led to us forming linkage agreements and memorandum of understandings. These external relationships brought more clients, more money which led to more locations. I was booming at work! I eventually became the head lady in charge. I was the executive assistant now. I was also a recovery home operator, office manager, and a National Certified Recovery Specialist (NCRS). My pockets were swollen and I was feeling good.

The lessons:
You cannot have relationship without reciprocity ~ Bishop T.D. Jakes

Bishop T.D. Jakes shares five steps to get a grip on your marriage:
Art of Knowing
Art of Listening
Art of Waiting
Art of Forgiving
Art of Openness

You may wonder what does working at a recovery home have to do with marriage. I mention this particular point now because this is where I met my second husband, the young man who I love dearly. He has taught me how to love when it is not the ideal marriage. We have not made this love thang easy and I now understand that love in itself matter of fact unconditional love is complex and challenging.
Love is a choice. Unconditional love is a commitment no matter what it looks like. Let me add, there are circumstances that causes us to terminate a relationship that we may have once deemed as love. Be mindful and make the right decision by taking whatever the circumstance(s) is to God.
There is unity in the Union. Sounds simple. Common sense. Right? Many people just don't get this concept. Maybe the reason your vision is in seclusion is because you have to change the way you interact with your spouse. Our day of unity started on August 8, 2012 to this present day. I have to publically apologize to my husband. I had too much baggage and he had his share of baggage too. But, the same mistreatment my ex-husband displayed was what I brought to

my current marriage. I played the games and tried to use word to cut into his soul. Sad. Sad. Sad. I am glad we were able to survive that.

We went on to run the recovery home as if it was our own. We brainstormed ideas and were on the forefront of all initiatives. We both decided to go back to school and complete our associate degree. I grew restless at South Suburban College and transferred to Governors State University (GSU). My boss agreed to my schedule change to accommodate my academic goals. The closer I came to completing my bachelor's degree (not an associate's) the more distant my relationship with my boss grew.

I had given my all to this organization. I was full-time worker who was also on call when emergencies occurred. Hell, I almost lost my life a few times being caught in heated discussions that resulted into a physical fight. There were times I locked myself in the office with my children because we had a deadline to meet for a grant or preparing for an audit. But, I took the position for granted and I never had a back-up plan. I thought I was the brains of the operation and could not be touched. Yeah! Okay! That's what I thought.

Never get too comfortable that you lack preparation for the next level. Never get so caught up in yourself that you lose yourself in the process. The more you grind and hustle for your employer means you have just as much work to do for yourself. Don't settle.

I finished my undergraduate studies on December 1, 2011. As I am out celebrating with some of my fellow students, I get a phone call that one of my dear friends was killed in his own home. We are talking about a young man who served our Country completing two tours and loses his life on his own turf. I won't go any further into that because his murder is still not solved. Bitter sweet moment.

Now that I found my flow in academics, I apply for the Criminal Justice graduate program. Admitted! Woot! Woot!

I'm doing so well that the young man in my life (now husband) decides to transfer from his community college to GSU. He completed his undergraduate degree May 2015.

I was not the best employee but I was ideal.

I think my boss and I had a father/daughter relationship that should have never happened. To this day, I can hear him call my name, "Shanique!" Not Shaniqua but Shanique. Ha!

December 9, 2011, was my friend's funeral. I am sitting in the church trying to process what is happening and why. The funeral was like a reunion for some and a reminder for others that our neighborhood ain't s$%^. One of ours was killed in his own home. These were our stomping grounds and someone knows something. Someone knows everything that happened. Bitter sweet moment.

So, I'm sitting there trying to be tough knowing damn well I was too messed up. I had taken off work for the day since I knew I was going to reunite with my childhood friends. I knew I was going to the cemetery which is something I typically don't do but this case was rare. My boss texted me. He's asking me if I was coming in to work. Uh! No! I have the day off, remember? He replies to my text and states that I am fired and I am no longer needed. What? You didn't even have the decency to fire me face-to-face. Maybe it was the right thing to do because face-to-face could have gotten out of control. I was angry. I was dealing with other emotions. I could not even comprehend what happened.

I never got a response as to the reason why. It's all good. Alignment. God knew my time had expired and even through the hurt and struggle, I survived. My boss' actions fueled my comeback. Not a temporary comeback but the full throttle, permanent comeback. I had never known what it was to apply for unemployment. The extended waiting period caused us to lose our apartment. We faced homelessness.

While some may say I was never homeless because I was welcomed into my mother's home. What you do not understand is that I was not married to my husband at the time and my God-fearing mother did not approve of us shacking nor allowed us to live under her roof together as "boyfriend" and "girlfriend." I was not going to turn my back on him so I hung tight. There were nights where I slept in the back room where the babies slept as well but for the most part, we slept in his van, my car, or rented a hotel room. The babies loved it because they thought we were living the life. They just did not know.

We were homeless the entire summer of 2012. I was entering my second semester of my graduate program and taking showers in the locker room. We stayed at GSU until we were told to leave by Department of Public Safety (DPS). Although, they never questioned why we were always on campus, some knew something was not right. We made it through that along with all the other circumstances. August 8th, 2012, we made it official.

While I learned the ropes, the highs, and the lows of operating a male recovery home, I also know that you have to stay focused on your mission. Whether that mission is associated with an organization or your life's mission, you have to stay focused. They say hurt people, hurt people.

I say people that have been helped, help people.

Chapter Ten

1 University Parkway

Why are we loyal to ineffectiveness? ~ T.D. Jakes

I had to learn over the course of time as a student transitioning into a professional that I can no longer live by tradition when my character as a person does not equate to such mediocrity. I am unique. I am a challenge all by myself and I take pride in knowing that I am different. I am a creative soul that seeks to make the lives of those I encounter brighter. I have been on the dark side and refuse to live according to my past. Ineffectiveness stops NOW!

I made every attempt to obtain an associate's degree from South Suburban Community College but there were one too many distractions and no focus.

You've got 86,400 seconds today. Have you used a second to say, thank you? ~ Shaniqua Jones

Governors State University is located in University Park, Illinois where their mission is: Governors State University is committed to offering an exceptional and accessible education that imbues students with the knowledge, skills, and confidence to succeed in a global society. GSU is dedicated to creating an intellectually stimulating public square, serving as an economic catalyst for the region and being a model of diversity and responsible citizenship.

I need you to understand the difference this public square has made in my life. I want to share my full speech as the 2013 Governors State University Commencement Speaker representing the College of Arts and Sciences & College of Business and Public Administration (now College of Business as of fall 2015):

THE JOURNEY

First giving honor to God who is the author and finisher of my faith. President Maimon, Board of Trustees, noble guests, and the graduating class of 2013, I thank you. I thank you for this moment to represent our student body this evening as we close one chapter and embark on a new journey. This journey began long before our initial decision to become a vested student of Governors State University (GSU). We were destined to be here and cross paths. We ran the race. We endured to the end...the end of one era and heading towards new successes the moment we step outside this facility.

In 1993-94, I was a participant of Economic Achievers: Inroads to Success at Governors State University. I was an 8th grader at Gwendolyn Brooks Middle School in Harvey, Illinois preparing for high school. At the end of our program, we had an award ceremony in the Hall of Honors where our talents were individually and collectively recognized. On that night, I told my mother I would return to GSU. In my mind, I thought I was going to leave Harvey, Illinois for two years after high school to receive my Aassociate degree in Journalism and return home to complete my bachelor's degree at GSU. Life did not happen the way I had planned.

Not really understanding the magnitude of the words I spoke 20 years ago...I stand here before you. I stand here as a representatives of our determination and our adversities. I stand here proudly representing each one of us who paved our way from different walks of life, various views and values but all with the same goal; completing our respective degrees. Regardless of what our journeys consisted of, we made it! I encourage you to continue rising above mediocracy and aiming toward your next level. Whether your next level is to gain employment; start a family; continue your education; or to become a game changer in our global society; continue the journey!

Each one of us here today has a story, a story to be heard, and a story to be accepted. At GSU, our collective stories have enabled us to be a part of one of the most rewarding experiences as we participate in our commencement ceremony on today. Although the reward is ours, it took courage to overcome various obstacles.

Whether those obstacles were temporary yet felt like a life time, we have overcome. I can recall times where I have cried and questioned my own ability to make it to this point. I know the sacrifices many of us made to be here from sleepless nights to study, childcare and employment accommodations to seeking assistance through the writing center or tutoring services. And oh those group projects!

As I stand here before you today, I represent my parents who sought to obtain a degree but the pressures of life prevented them from exceeding their educational expectations. I represent my five children who diligently display a life of academia within their studies, who offered unconditional love and support, understood my need to work on assignments and allowed me study time, and consoled me daily. I represent my soul mate who took a vow; not only to our marriage but to excel academically and partake in this educational bond. I represent the fear we had to overcome to walk in our destiny, the self-doubt we may have possessed of achieving success, the societal stigmas, and the excuses of allowing our past such space in determining my fate.

Attending GSU to me is more than obtaining a degree for personal and financial gain but to find passion, give back to our communities, build lasting relationships, and create solutions to the societal issues we discussed in our classes. As college graduates, we are here because we endured to the end of the beginning. Today is the beginning of a legacy, a new journey and goals that are tangible. The obstacles and challenges were all a part of this journey. During this process, we learned our purpose. We learned who we are as individuals and what we have to offer this global society by providing our knowledge and ideas formulated throughout our educational experience here at GSU. We have been molded and shaped by our professors, advisors, fellow students, and other support staff to hone our  skills and leave a lasting impression on all those we encounter. On today, I salute you, the leader and the voice of those unheard, The Graduating Class of 2013!!!

Earlier that year (January 2013), my husband and I had the opportunity to partake in history as we attended the Presidential Inauguration with other GSU students, faculty, and staff. This was a rewarding experience. Thank you GSU!

If you don't know, now you know.....

I am Shaniqua Jones; wife, mother of ten children (five by marriage), full-time employee and student. The passion to be a shareholder in higher education began as a student worker at South Suburban College over 10 years ago. During my journey of achieving my academic goals, I stumbled a few times due to extenuating life circumstances.

The greatness occurred when I continued this journey exceeding my initial academic goals of obtaining an associate or bachelor's degree. After attending South Suburban College intermittently for over 10 years with no degree in hand, I decided to attend an Instant Decision Day at Governors State University in summer 2010 with five active children by my side.

I received my bachelor's degree fall 2011 in Interdisciplinary Studies. From there, I applied and was admitted into the Criminal Justice Master's program. In 2012, I received a graduate assistantship in the Criminal Justice Master's Program at Governors State University. From that moment on, my life began to  elevate to prominence. I completed the program as a high academic scholar and was nominated as the 2013 Governors State University Commencement Speaker. I never imagined coming to a place of humbleness and gratitude for education which led to this very moment.

Here I am, mother of ten children who has struggled her entire adulthood, financially and medically to make ends meet, stands before an auditorium filled with over 2,000 people and  nationally streamed live as the commencement speaker representing the entire graduating class of 2013. One of the highlights of the graduate program experience transpired during my capstone project. Along with another graduate student and professor, we created a 15-credit hour, 5 course Restorative Justice Certificate program for undergraduate, and graduate students, and community members.

The main objective is to provide each individual with the knowledge to apply restorative approaches in their capacity  (home, community, school, work, etc.). Applicants must have a successful record of upper division college course work. April 2014, I had the opportunity to coordinate and co-chair a regional Restorative Justice Drive-In Conference to create a dialogue involving restorative practices in various dimensions.

The ability to apply theory to practice occurred when I learned of a philosophy, restorative justice in the master's program. Restorative justice in higher education is a personal passion to build social capital particularly in a four-year institution. The intent is to create a unique position as Associate Dean of Student Affairs implementing restorative practices within the campus community. Achieving intended goals will consist of: allowing shareholders involved in specific offenses/violations the opportunity to resolve an issue in a restorative manner (i.e. circle, conference, mediation); provide a safe and comfortable environment to all shareholders involved within an infraction; ensure that there is a strategic plan in place to administer follow-up within a timely manner; address underlying issues in an authentic approach to resolve issues; and provide an array of resources to all shareholders based on the dynamic of needs.

As a doctoral student I was appointed the Restorative Justice Consultant for the Governors State University Student Conduct Committee and privileged to teach the inaugural first-year students this past academic semester. With the support of the Governors State University community, the ability to implement restorative practices sets GSU apart from other higher education institutions processes in place to build social capital and/or resolve conflicts. I had the honor to be selected

as one of eight Mastering College Success courses designed for first-year students this past fall 2014. The opportunity to teach in a non-traditional manner was granted and initiated meaningful relationships with first-year students.

Restorative justice is a philosophy that encourages meaningful dialogue among shareholders within a safe space. In other matters, restorative justice is utilized to resolve conflict between all parties involved without placing blame on what one may consider the 'offender'. Restorative justice seeks to resolve the root cause(s) in order to prevent any reoccurrences.

Weitekamp (1999) provided a vigorous statement "restorative justice has existed since humans began forming communities" (p. 81). He says, "It is kind of ironic that we have to go back to methods and forms of conflict resolution that were practiced some millennia ago by our ancestors who seemed to be much more successful than we are today." (p. 93).

Restorative justice relies less on traditional judicial processing, and more on victim, community, and reprobate-centered practices that hold individuals who have caused harm accountable for their actions. Restorative justice practices ensure that the consequences of harms and offenses meet the specific needs and desires of victims and community members, while attending to improvement in the individual who have caused harm competencies so as to prevent future harmful behavior on the wrongdoer's part.

DISPEL THE STIGMA(S)

I am an African-American woman who has kept the term underrepresented at the forefront of my mission to dispel the stigma associated with being an individual essentially defined atypical. Leading with this mission in mind, my personal and professional goals influence others through sharing my journey. We all have a journey with evocative dialogue awaiting the moment to share the process to success. Oftentimes, many focus on the success alone without regard to the process taken to achieve success. The other factor to address is the way one may define success; typically defined by personal experiences and aspirations.

Not only am I an African-American woman, my name is Shaniqua. The negative connotation that comes along with my first name only drives me to excel to higher heights and deeper depths. I have embarked on a journey to know who I am and what I represent in terms of my identity. As the biological mother of four young ladies and one young man, I must acknowledge the journey in the most authentic way. I am no longer ashamed to speak in a room full of scholars for I am a life scholar. Challenges and obstacles created a passion to assist others in the process of restoration.

We can no longer accept the terms and conditions of societal factors hindering our ability to progress in a matter feasible to our existence. Restoration is vital for our progress. In higher education, shareholders must have a safe place to speak from the heart to appreciate their experiences.

A true appreciation for your personal journey will equip you for the road to come. Teaching the Governors State University Mastering College Success course in a non-traditional manner has strengthened the bond with my former students. This course is mandatory for all first-year students that should be made mandatory across the board for all students of every academic level. This one class alone can prepare a student for the academic and professional roles ahead. I am proud to facilitate this process enabling students to achieve and excel in life.

I had the honor to speak at the Governors State University Inclusive Leadership Conference on January 23, 2015. For several weeks prior to the conference, I had prepared notes with highlighted focal points connecting leadership to destiny. As many notes and practice runs to hear the words that were going to flow from my mouth, my speech turned into a testimony. With the bright lights shining down on me as I stood at the podium glancing at the audience consisting of scholars who had paved the way for me, I spoke my truth.

My truth is that there was a time when I allowed pressure to consume me. I thought the only way to be accepted was to fit in when I was clearly made to stand out. Raised in single-family household where at one point my mother struggled to make ends meet and our dinner consisted of sharing a pack of noodles, I learned early on to take trying times as a lesson. Opposed to going away to school, I decided to attend a community college since I was afraid to step outside my comfort zone. Although I struggled academically due to allowing outside forces to impact my decision-making skills, here I am today completing a doctoral degree.

In all my years, I came to the conclusion that there is no growth in your comfort. The moment I stepped outside my comfort zone, I began to live the life I was destined from the time I entered this world. The chains I was bound down by were broken on the day when I began to delve into sharing my journey with all open to listen. My mission is to provide the space for underrepresented individuals to be empowered through acknowledging their truth, their journey.

TO MY BABIES:

I've never been one to sugarcoat anything with you and can sometimes feel as if I've said too much. I don't regret my realness in hopes of preparing you for what your friends and naysayers (who can be one in the same) have to say. Don't let their words and experiences cause you to make irrational decisions that will affect you for the rest of your life. The golden rule is to treat people how you want to be treated. A more appropriate rule is the platinum rule to treat people how they want to be treated. Everyone doesn't want to be treated like you, so act accordingly. It's never too late.....for

anything. Learning never ends and comes in many forms. Accept and expect change. It happens.

Believe in the fact that you appreciate more when you work for it. Don't take anything we consider simple or complex for that matter, for granted. What's given easily is taken away in the same manner. Work my child! Find your passion while you're in school. Listen carefully and follow your gut feelings. Stand strong and don't waiver from what you believe.

Let's take a minute and talk about appearance and presentation. It's everything! If you don't care to keep yourself up, how do you expect others to genuinely respect you? You're far more intelligent than you give yourself credit for. The problem is that you've created this box....a box that has walls....limits. Throw the damn box away baby! Being loud and loose only presents problems for you. There is no need to act as if you have no home training. You'll get further in life when you learn to listen, observe, and remain humble.

There is no need to lie. Lying is too much work and causes you to become frustrated and overwhelmed. You are setting yourself up for failure when attempting to live a fraudulent life.

Reference
Weitekamp, E. (1999). The History of Restorative Justice. In G. Bazemore & L. Walgrave (Eds.), Restorative Juvenile Justice: Repairing the Harm of Youth
Crime (pp. 75-102). New York: Criminal Justice Press.

I AM **SHANIQUA**

BORN IN **HARVEY, IL**

MADE WITH **HONOR & TRUTH**

I AM **ODIA'S** DAUGHTER

#BORNandMADE

Chapter Eleven

BLACK LIVES MATTER

One of the most profound revelations I received was that even the people that are with me will alienate me because they do not see my vision. More importantly, they do not see the predestined vision God has set for me. The reality is that the vision is NOT for "them" to see. God did not give the vision to them. He gave the vision to ME!

I know I have mentioned God quite a bit in my memoir. I am fine with it. Are you? I

know I am not too religious; and definitely not religious at all to the point that I miss the revelation.

If you have taken this journey with me, you are conscious that I have experienced poverty and homelessness.

My poverty activates my prosperity. I did not know what it was to go through until I went through and I came out victorious.

Faith is the substance of things hoped for and the evidence of things not seen. ~ Hebrews 11:1

God's Response to Injustice

John 5:1-8

The Healing at the Pool

Sometime later, Jesus went up to Jerusalem for one of the Jewish festivals. Now there in Jerusalem near the Sheep Gate is a pool, which in Aramaic is called Bethesda and is surrounded by five covered colonnades. Here a great number of disabled people used to (lie)??—the blind, the lame, the paralyzed. One who was there had been an invalid for thirty-eight years. When Jesus saw him lying there and learned that he had been in this condition for a long time, he asked him, "Do you want to get well?" "Sir," the invalid replied, "I have no one to help me into the pool when the water is stirred. While I am trying to get in, someone else goes down ahead of me." Then Jesus said to him, "Get up! Pick up your mat and walk."

In this passage Jesus showed up and began to ask questions. You can't keep quiet. Dealing with an injustice means we have to ask the tough questions. We were not called to be passive.

There is no healing in your silence.

My pastor shared a sermon on the Kingdom's response to injustice on April 4, 2015, after the death of Walter Scott. He mentioned three things we should do as Christians when an injustice occurs:

Show up

Speak up

Stand up

You cannot conquer what you can't confront ~ Pastor Moses Herring

I once attended monthly prayer at my mom's home for a short period of time. I was given the task of bringing the Word on November 7, 2015.

The Word came from a personal place. Insurance vs. Assurance with supporting scripture; Luke 21:14-19 "Settle it therefore in your hearts, not to meditate before what ye shall answer. For I will give you a mouth and wisdom which all your adversaries shall not be able to gainsay nor resist. And ye shall be betrayed both by parents and brethren, and Kinsfolks, and friends, and some of you shall they cause to be put to death. And ye shall be hated of all men for my name's sake.

But there shall not a hair of your head perish. In your patience possess ye your soul."

According to Merriam-Webster, Assurance means a strong and definite statement that something will happen or that something is true while insurance means of guaranteeing protection or safety. With insurance, the moment you stop paying the monetary price, protection ends. You are no longer covered and you are held liable. When Jesus paid it all, He provided everlasting assurance. There is no better coverage than the coverage Jesus provides.

Stop asking God for minute things! He's bigger than that! Why ask to rent when you can own? The size of your faith is a reflection of your request. ~ SJ

What are you asking God for? My next question is, which is even more important, what are you doing for God? Too often, we are asking Him to work on our behalf when we are not even willing to make a move. I am willing to put the work in and I know everything will be alright.

On December 31, 2015, at Faith Movers Church in University Park, IL during our New Year's Eve service, God spoke loud and clear to me:

I'm sitting in service and it felt as if someone tapped me to get my attention. God spoke loud and clear to me and I'm sharing with you.

Don't enter another year of your life having an affair with God. He's not your secret or go-to when you're in distress only. Have an authentic reciprocal relationship with Him.

God is....

#SayHerName – Sandra Bland

There are times where we question our calling and how we can insure we channel the right message. There are times when we feel helpless and hopeless as we grieve one travesty to only face an even more disheartening injustice. In Sandy's death, she speaks volumes as we are compelled and moved to action. I am hurt. I am grieving. I am.

There have been other ridiculous instances of precious lives being lost to racism, sexism, and power along with other – isms. Unfortunately, these same lives were only precious to those who deemed the term  suitable while others coined these lives to be inconsequential. The tragic death [murder] of Sandra Bland struck the last social injustice nerve that I had in my interior. Have you ever felt so connected to a tragedy that others thought you may have had a personal encounter with the precious soul? When a tragedy hits close to home whether it is in terms of similarities; she's Black, I'm Black; she's educated, I'm educated; striving to work in higher education, so am I; both can be mouthy; "stand for something or fall for anything" type of gals; unfortunate run-in with the law (my cases ended differently); social media presence reflects the social ills of our communities...I can go on and on.

I do not discredit the precious lives of: Betty Jones (Chicago, IL.), Tamir Rice (Cleveland, OH.), Walter Scott (North Charleston, SC.), Michael Brown (Ferguson, MO.), LaQuan McDonald (Chicago, IL.), Trayvon Martin (Miami Gardens, FL.), (executed) Troy Davis (Georgia Department of

Corrections), Eric Garner (Staten Island, NY.), Oscar Grant (Oakland, CA.), Freddie Gray (Baltimore, MD.), and many more in my time as being a restorative and social justice advocate.

Her mission as a breathing and fearless individual was to tackle social injustices. In her death, she has managed to spark a fire in those, such as myself, to become more involved in the "movement", to become more conscious of our reality, to not only become or remain social media poster children and in hiding behind electronic screens but to become engaged and doers of this generation for the generations to come. A young man I admire said, "What side of history will you be on? The side that sat on the sideline as demonstrators actively exercised their rights or the side that made moves in the right direction."

A Texas state trooper who arrested Sandra Bland after a contentious traffic stop last summer was fired Wednesday after being charged with perjury for allegedly lying about his confrontation with the black woman who died three days later in jail. "I'm thrilled to see that they've acknowledged what we saw 5 1/2 to 6 months ago that the police officer lied," said Bland's sister Sharon Cooper.
- Fox 32 News posted January 6, 2016; updated January 7, 2016.

***

A Texas state trooper was charged with perjury on Wednesday in connection to the contentious traffic stop last summer where Sandra Bland wound up arrested for assault and then died three days later in jail.
A grand jury indicted Trooper Brian Encinia with the misdemeanor count, alleging he lied about how he removed the 28-year-old, formerly of Naperville, from her vehicle during the July traffic stop. The same Waller County grand jury decided last month not to indict any sheriff's officials or jailers in Bland's death, which was ruled a suicide. Bland remained jailed following her arrest because she couldn't raise about $500 for bail. Encinia, who has been on paid desk duty since Bland was found dead in her jail cell, also faces a wrongful death lawsuit filed by Bland's family. The misdemeanor charge carries

a maximum penalty of a year in jail and a
$4,000 fine.
- Chicago Tribune January 6, 2015

***

A grand jury has decided not to indict anyone in
the jailhouse death of Sandra Bland.
Prosecutors say the grand jury will reconvene to
discuss whether or not to charge the officer who
arrested Bland before she was found dead in her
Texas jail cell.
- Asbury Park Press December 21, 2015

***

"I'm the mama, and I'm telling you that my baby
did not take herself out," Geneva Reed-Veal,
Bland's mother, said at the memorial service.
Bland, 28, DIED [REALLY?] in Prairie View on
July 13 -- three days after she was arrested for
noncompliance toward a Texas state trooper
and thrown in jail. Police said she was stopped
because she failed to signal a lane change.
Bland, however, thought the trooper's actions
were excessive -- which led to an altercation,
and the arrest.
- United Press international July 25, 2015

***

Her death has sparked the latest national debate about police treatment of black people, with hashtags such as #WhatHappenedToSandraBland trending nationally on Twitter. Bland was found hanging in a "semi standing position with the ligature surrounding her neck," according to the sheriff's office statement. She was hanging from a "privacy partition" in the cell, according to the statement.
- Chicago Tribune July 21, 2015

***

RESTORATIVE JUSTICE

I would love to be a philanthropist and this is exactly what I am working towards. A philanthropist is one who seeks to promote the welfare of others, especially by the generous  donation of money to good causes (Merriam-Webster). I plan to give whatever God allows. I know my work in restorative justice is not in vain.

I chose the side that makes moves in the right direction. One of my passions is the philosophy of Restorative Justice; in particular, one of the practices, Talking Circles. The Talking Circle is a restorative practice that provides a safe, non-judgmental place to discuss the matter at hand which is either proactive or reactive in nature.

Chapter 10 focuses on my experience at Governors State University. During this rewarding experience, I had the opportunity to be mentored by one of the greatest instructors in higher education, Dr. James Coldren whom I call my Caucasian father. Don't judge. He introduced me to this philosophy when I was a student and graduate assistant. I worked with other students and external organizations to gain a better understanding of restorative justice and how to utilize these tools in their various capacities.

Man! I wish the folks who were handling my misdemeanor "situations" knew about this philosophy. I wish those Godly people who turned their backs on me knew about restorative justice.....Oh wait! They did. They claimed to have lived a righteous life and followed God. Ha! That's not me being bitter. This is me being real, maybe too real. I doubt it.

Back to restorative justice. In my opinion, students will not  fully understand or grasp the concept taught until applied in a real-life situation; applying theory to practice. Here I am co-teaching and networking as an advocate for restorative justice when my reality happened. My oldest daughter was in junior high school at the time when she frantically calls me informing me that she might have to fight after getting off the after school bus. The phone hangs up. I immediately grab my keys and fly out the door. Mind you, I am leaving University Park driving to Harvey as fast as I can.

As I am driving, she calls me on numerous occasions while I am doing the best I can to get to her yelling to the top of her lungs that she had to fight, the girl she fought grandmother jumped in, and that she was being chased by the girl and her family. The last phone call...the call dropped.

I'm yelling. I'm cursing. I'm praying. (Repeat)

By the time I get to her, one of my childhood friends had come to her rescue and fought the crowd off. The police arrived and began to question my daughter of all the details. By the incident initially occurring on the after school bus, the school was notified of the incident as well. This is when I arose to the occasion because I was on fire and had to find the calm in the midst of the storm.

A police report was filed and all parties involved had to meet with school administration the next morning. The hype was that I was going to go off on a tangent and that this was going to be an ongoing issue at the school as well as in the neighborhood. There was additional police on school grounds the day we all had to meet. There was a part of me that wanted to revert back to old ways but I was reminded that those same old ways kept me in bondage. I took the highest  road possible. I entered the room in gratitude, knowing the situation could have escalated to great injury including death.

I asked the administration if they had ever heard of the philosophy, restorative justice and its various practices. Ironically, the school principal' previous position at a high school was heavily involved with the work. His approach and tone changed from that point on where we all were able to address the underlying issues, hash out differences, come to an agreement, and move forward (with caution though). I love the Lord but I will come for you when it comes to mine. I'm just playing. No, I'm not. There were other consequences handled by law enforcement and we were ultimately pleased with the outcome.

Restorative justice is an alternative approach to specific punitive situations that causes for parties to confront demons. This is me taking a spiritual approach to help you understand why I love restorative justice so much. Now, how can we operate as believers, yet be so set to turn all the way up on our neighbor for the pettiest occurrences. I (we) have to do a better job of holding each other accountable and building meaningful and lasting relationships. Restorative justice is a way of life and each life should be respected to the fullest extent. Yeah! Some people would never honor this philosophy because they either have not reached a level of maturity to do so or they are committed to creating and continuing havoc by any means.
Do what works for you, Boo! For real.

BLACK LIVES MATTER

Patrisse Cullors along with co-founders, Alicia Garza and Opal Tometi built this Black Lives Matter movement. Tometi shared with Huffington Post that she was inspired by Alicia Garza's post on social media that the anger people felt was justified and that "black lives matter." Patrisse Cullors added the hashtag to these three significant words and began to continuously post as a hashtag (#BlackLivesMatter) which sparked the creation of this platform.

To learn more and to join the movement, go to:
http://blacklivesmatter.com

I despise the nature in which people address #AllLivesMatter, degrading the many precious lives of Black people lost to racial divide and lack of concern for Blacks, male, female, young or elder. We all know all lives matter and as a God-fearing woman, I am able to articulate the difference of those treated like lepers while others are treated with the highest level of value.

NOW THAT I HAVE GIVEN MY TWO CENTS, WHAT DO YOU PLAN ON DOING?

WHAT SIDE OF HISTORY WILL YOU BE ON?

LEAVE A LEGACY. MAKE A LASTING IMPACT.

If you share and teach others what God has given you, you live forever.

THE BOTTOM LINE

BLACK LIVES MATTER

Chapter Twelve

THE BOOK OF PROVERBS

The men stole my heart.

The book of Proverbs was said to be written by Solomon, the son of David who became king of Israel. Solomon's request to God was to give him the wisdom to walk upright before God, an understanding of how he will accomplish the tasks at hand and the knowledge to guide His people. Because of Solomon's request, God gave him everything he asked for and some. God gave Solomon riches as well. Solomon was the richest man in that particular section of the world.  Solomon was young, good looking and a man after God's own heart. Solomon was given 700 wives and 300 concubines. Solomon was a good king but after so long, the women stole his heart.

The date is Friday, December 4, 2015, approximately 10:30pm (CST). I am sitting in the living room with my mother and begin to tell her how God has been dealing with me as I complete this memoir. I tell her how busy life has been and how I needed to make time to read my Word on a more consistent basis. I go on to explain how God gave me the book of Proverbs after answering my prayer in giving me the exact word for me. At first, I couldn't understand if God was giving me instructions on how I need to carry myself as a woman of God or if this was some form of a discipline for me. Either way, I needed more clarity. And then this moment happened where my mother and I began to converse about my past and my relationship with God.

After breaking the book of Proverbs down to me and sharing the goodness of God, we both shared a profound moment. I had allowed the men to steal my heart. I strayed from the goodness of God to find something in the world. I turned into this promiscuous young woman who had come to the conclusion that my happiness was in men. I chose men over God. I thought the temporary lustful emotions and idea of happiness would lead me to the happiness I was in search

of when I was a little girl. I allowed men to enter my body and have their way with me thinking that the only way to find true love was through the loins.

I allowed the men I slept with or had adorned as the ones I knew God did not send to me create a wedge between me and

my God. From birth, my mother was my role model and I was her protégé. I was called Lil' Missionary from the time I could comprehend to the age of 15; right before I began to rebel. I sought God for myself and tithed without a second thought. God was not a game to me. He was everything. I wanted to live for Him and bless His people with the blessings He had bestowed upon me. We may not have had much but I was grateful because He made a way when my mother and I were struggling to make ends meet. I watched prayers being answered. I witnessed miracles before my very eyes. I read my word daily for an understanding of who He was and how I can use His word to strengthen the relationship I had with Him. I lived for Him. I walked the straight and narrow path and asked God for forgiveness because I knew we as humans sinned on a daily basis.

I know I was not the perfect child but I knew who God was and knew He held my future. I was an old soul. I mentioned how I did not have a choice in the matter when it came to being with my mother, aunt, and one of the oldest missionaries of the congregation. Honestly, my walk with God and being with the older saints was my safe place. Being a child of God was my security from the ills of this world. No, it didn't mean that I would live a life free from hardships but it did mean that whatever situation that came to challenge me would be my testimony of victory. The men stole my heart.

First, there was the young man I lost my virginity to at the age of 15. I lost my virginity Christmas of 1995. I had spent the night at a friend's home and slept with her cousin. We did not have a relationship and a relationship should have been the furthest thing from my mind but I had begun my search for that "thing". This is a contribution of peer pressure. Everyone in my circle of friends talked day and night about boys and having these sexual relationships. They talked in detail of all the things that they had done. Now, here I am with baby formula behind my ears trying to stay with the conversation. I was so lost but what I had gathered was that I was the last of the squad to be a virgin. That's when the search began but I was torn between two forces; the force of the world and God's way. I chose the world because I was too ashamed to admit I had made a mistake. I allowed my pride from returning to the life I lived prior to my rebellion.

I had turned into someone I did not even recognize. No glasses. No nappy hair. Fake nails. Slimming down. I had a way with words that was intriguing to the opposite sex. I was ready....or so I thought. I thought I was too slick and cute. My smile was contagious and I was a socialite in ways I couldn't even comprehend. I gave this young man something precious and something that should have been treasured and saved until the one God sent came along.

That was one of the worst experiences I ever had. Unfortunately, there were more similar to that experience. There was no relationship but a lustful attachment that I sought after. We used protection. It did not last longer than a series of holiday commercials that I could here in the background. I felt so disgusting that I ran into the bathroom and cried like a baby. I stared in the mirror trying to look deep into the eyes of the little girl who stood in the mirror. She was gone. Forever. I did a disservice to myself.

The next day, I went home and showered thinking I could wipe away my sins from the previous night. Have you ever watched one of those Lifetime movies and the person who is in distraught is showering as if they had been violated? It was possible that the character may have been violated. This violation was personal. The young man did not violate me. I gave him permission to enter my sacred place. I gave him an open invitation. When I saw my girls, I had a story to tell. I told them every ill-fated detail yet I added passion to the script in hopes of igniting further inquiry. After sharing all the details their questions were not in congruence with their previous conversations. I started to sweat profusely because the stories were not adding up.

After gathering the words to ask the boiling question, I asked, "Did ya play me?" In so many words, they played your girl. The two that meant the most to me as friends, had NEVER had sex. They were still virgins. I played it off. I kept my emotions to myself because when it's all said and done the decision I made was a personal choice. I wanted to get out there and search for that "thing". I thought I was grown and who was going to stop me? This is my body.

The men stole my heart. This was just the beginning to a 10-year battle of addiction to affection, lust, and lies.

THE WOMAN AT THE WELL

Two cap off the need and direction in writing this memoir, I went to church that Sunday, December 6, 2015, and the pastor's message was about the woman at the well. Well, let me tell you how insightful this message was. The message was read from the book of John 4: 5-30. The woman at the well was a Samaritan who showed no respect for a person who so happen to be Jesus. She questioned Jesus as being a Jew. His  request for water was peculiar. During the conversation, Jesus spoke of natural water and spiritual water. The natural water would only give her temporary satisfaction. She will be thirsty again within the same hour. Yet, the spiritual water will give her an everlasting quench. She'll thirst no more.

What I appreciated about my pastor's teaching was that he delivered the message in a way I never comprehended before. I've heard the story of the woman at the well a million times over but not like this. It's something about the promises of God when you give Him an earnest request. The moment I gave it all to Him, He brought life to dead situations. He provided clarity on situations I thought I had understood. He cleansed my spiritual lenses so I could see clearly.

The woman lied to Jesus when He asked her about her husband. Not only did she have five ex-husbands she also had a new boo she was shacking with. Now the woman knew that Jesus was not the ordinary guy and that there was something special about Him that she could not explain. What I did not know was that the woman was at the well for something other than water. She was in search of another man. The time of day that she was at the well is known to be the time the men were at the well. The conversation continues on to the point that the woman mentions the Messiah.

He informs the woman that He is the Messiah. In her exhilaration, the woman went to find the men leaving her water jar behind.

My pastor covered a series called, Reprogram for 2015 that positioned us to cover the lesson regarding the woman at the well. See the woman had to be reprogramed in order to receive what Jesus had in store for her. To be reprogrammed, my pastor says three things had to change: 1) attitude; 2) appetite; and 3) assignment.

Initially, she did not want to hear anything Jesus had to say nor respected His presence. She sought and starved for the attention of a man to feel a void. She had set forth on a quest to fulfill her appetite not knowing her encounter with Jesus was going to change her life.

God has a way of coming into your life when He sees that you are on a quest of destruction. He will encounter you to expose you in front of you and you alone. He will gain your attention through the truth you denied for so long. He will use you as a vessel to show that if your life can be restored, anyone can receive the same opportunity.

GET WISDOM, GET UNDERSTANDING; DO NOT FORGET MY WORDS OR TURN AWAY FROM THEM. ~ PROVERBS 4:5

I've said this one too many times before but not with this much emphasis. This time, I hope this message moves you.
Thinking outside the box allows you to have the option to revert back to the box when times seem unbearable.

Destroy the box. ~ SJ 12/20/2015

Shaniqua Jones

Shaniqua Jones, a leader in her own right and a proven professional of high standards within the post-secondary arena. Among other responsibilities, she is the Navy College Program for Afloat College Education Coordinator and Staff Clerk for the School of Extended Learning and the Office of International Services at Governors State University (GSU).

Shaniqua began her professional career in the non-profit sector on the south side of Chicago for several years. During this time, she was promoted from office assistant to executive assistant and recovery home operator over three male recovery homes. She formed lasting relationships with a variety of state agencies ranging from Cook County Drug Court, Chicago Department of Public Health, Illinois Department of Human Services, and Illinois Department of Corrections.

Shaniqua transitioned to entrepreneurship as the CEO of Senorita Entertainment providing a welcoming experience for comedians and patrons to partake in fellowship and laughter in the south suburban Cook County area. The platform allowed local comics to hone their skills while nationally recognized comedians returned to an intimate setting to perform. Shaniqua saw the need to be more creative in approach to promoting local talent by combining a vendor experience for small business owners.

As Shaniqua completed her undergraduate and graduate degree at Governor State University (GSU), she learned of the philosophy of Restorative Justice under the leadership of her mentor and professor. Restorative Justice became a way of life for her as she was able to apply theory to practice in her own personal affairs. Shaniqua was recognized as a student leader on campus by modeling the way and encouraging the heart. Even through facing hard times, Shaniqua managed to rise to the occasion. For her final project to complete her graduate degree, she co-created a 15-semester credit hour Restorative Justice Certificate Program. In 2013, Shaniqua graduated with her Master of Science in Criminal Justice as the Commencement Speaker which is one of the highest academic honors a student can achieve at GSU.

Her diverse background in academics and her profession as well as her personal journey has allowed her to understand the concerns of those she serve. As a current student, she has had the opportunity to serve the student body as a leader in addressing concerns, being visible and available, and supporting student-based programs on campus.

She is currently in the Interdisciplinary Leadership doctoral program due to graduate May 2016. She has become an active restorative and social justice advocate within higher education. Her passion for Restorative Justice has afforded her the opportunity to speak and present across the Chicagoland area on the proactive and reactive approaches regarding restorative practices such as, build meaningful relationships, promoting accountability, and operating in a safe environment.

She plans to start her own non-profit organization offering an outlet for youth to speak from the heart without judgment, however receiving support of their creative endeavors. She believes that we are support systems to one another and should exemplify social capital in terms of creating solutions and resolving issues internally. She also recognizes the importance of promoting sustainable consumption in higher education as a contribution to bridge the gap between service learning and subsidiary learning to maximize the academic experience for students as well as administration, faculty and staff.

Shaniqua understands that higher education plays a crucial role in the social development of young and returning adults to effectively face societal challenges, cultural diversity, and environmental issues – emphasizing civic engagement. With many colleges and universities moving towards a more civically engaged institution, the paradigm shift to focus on social justice and civic responsibility is becoming more prominent. To promote the social and economic development through service and incidental learning, WE must have the opportunity to be catalyst to enhance experiences through collaborative efforts. This quest is continued through Shaniqua's academic, professional and personal gains.

Made in the USA
Monee, IL
07 February 2021

58496469R00108